The Bismarc

AMERICA READS

Rediscovered Fiction and Nonfiction from Key Periods in American History

THE GREAT DEPRESSION

Little Napoleons and Dummy Directors (1933)
Being the Narrative of the Bank of United States

The Barter Lady (1934)
A Woman Farmer Sees It Through

The House of Dawn (1935)
A Novel

WORLD WAR II

The Island (1944)
A History of the First Marine Division on Guadalcanal

Robinson Crusoe, USN (1945)
The Adventures of George R. Tweed Rm1c on Japanese-Held Guam

The Bismarck Episode (1948)

THE BISMARCK EPISODE

RUSSELL GRENFELL

WESTHOLME
Yardley

Originally published in 1948 by Faber & Faber.

Westholme Publishing, LLC
Eight Harvey Avenue
Yardley, Pennsylvania 19067
Visit our Web site at www.westholmepublishing.com

First Printing: March 2010
10 9 8 7 6 5 4 3 2 1

ISBN: 978-1-59416-110-0

Printed in United States of America.

Contents

Appendices

Illustrations

Maps

Preface

The writing of this book was made possible by the kindness and unstinted help of numerous officers who took part in the operation and who have shown the utmost generosity in providing me with information about their own experiences therein.

My thanks are principally due to Admirals of the Fleet Lord Tovey and Sir James Somerville who, as the two chief Commanders afloat, have had to put up with the major share of my importunities. Of the considerable trouble they have both taken to put me right on many points of fact and to explain how the situation appeared to them at different periods of the operation I cannot make sufficient acknowledgment.

My indebtedness is only slightly less to Admiral Lord Fraser, Admiral Sir Percy Noble, Air Chief Marshal Sir Frederick Bowhill, Vice-Admirals Sir Rhoderick McGrigor, Sir Frederick Dalrymple-Hamilton, Sir Patrick Brind, Sir Philip Vian, Sir Wilfred Patterson, and H. C. Bovell, Rear-Admirals A. J. L. Phillips, L. E. H. Maund, R. A. B. Edwards, C. Caslon, C. M. Blackman, R. M. Servaes, and A. D. Read, Commodore C. A. A. Larcom, Captains H. M. Ellis, H. L. St. J. Fancourt, G. A. Rotherham, C. Coppinger, W. J. C. Robertson, C. Meynell, and P. V. Peyton-Ward, Captain (S) A. W. Pafford, Commanders C. McMullen, V. C. Grenfell, and A. G. Skipwith, Instructor-Commander C. Young, Lieutenants C. G. A. Murphy and G. A. G. Brooke, and Mrs. Tom Halsey. Owing to the non-publication of the Navy List, I have been unable to verify honours and decorations in all cases, and have therefore regretfully concluded it is best to leave them all out. I am simi-

Preface

larly beholden to Admiral Walter Gladisch, of the late German Navy, for the valuable information he kindly sent me about the action of 24th May 1941.

My grateful thanks are also due to the Air Ministry for all the ready help it gave me in connection with the part played by Coastal Command, and to the Admiralty for the answers to certain questions and for permission to publish a photograph not hitherto released: also to the Stationery Office regarding the Crown Copyright in this photograph, and in the extract from the official handbook, *Coastal Command*, given on page 135.

I am particularly grateful to the United States Navy Department for so courteously giving me information about the U.S. Coastguard Cutter *Modoc*.

R.G.

August 1948

CHAPTER 1

The First Alarm

In the middle of May 1941, Britain's fortunes were low. For practically a year she had been standing all by herself in face of the powerful and victorious Axis Powers: and there was so far no real indication that her loneliness would be ended. Hitler's forces had conquered Norway, Denmark, Holland, Belgium, and France in 1940. Early in 1941 they had overrun Yugoslavia and had passed on to the invasion of Greece. By the end of April, German troops had reached Cape Matapan and the country was in their hands. Crete was still in possession of Anglo-Greek forces, but information came in steadily during the early days of May of strenuous German activity in the south of Greece which pointed to an attack on the island being launched at an early date.

At sea, the situation was bad and getting worse. The acquisition by the enemy of the whole Norwegian coast and the French Channel and Atlantic seaboards had given him numerous excellent bases for the prosecution of his submarine offensive against shipping, an offensive which was facilitated by the grave shortages in convoy escort vessels and coastal aircraft with which Britain had entered the war and which could not be rectified under many months. Mercantile losses had been mounting ever since the fall of France. By May 1941, they had become so serious that the British War Cabinet was on the point of deciding that it would be contrary to the national interest to publish any more monthly figures of the tonnage sunk.

The German Naval Command was not content to rely only

on U-boats and aircraft, great as was the damage they were inflicting, but was using also its surface vessels in the attack on Britain's sea communications. The *Scheer* had been operating against shipping in the Atlantic late in 1940. The battle cruisers *Scharnhorst* and *Gneisenau* had been out early in 1941 and had inflicted some severe losses on convoys before appearing at Brest in March. It was almost certain, too, that the new battleship *Bismarck* had been completed and had for some months been under training in the Baltic. She also might take a hand in the game at any time.

By the third week in May, matters in the Eastern Mediterranean were warming up towards an obvious crisis. Air attacks on shipping and jetties in Suda Bay, the principal unloading port used by the Allied forces in Crete, increased steadily in intensity. Then, on 20th May, the news reached Whitehall that a German airborne invasion of Crete had begun that morning.

In the early hours of the next day, 21st May, a report arrived in the Admiralty to the effect that two large German warships, heavily screened and accompanied by eleven merchant vessels, had been seen steaming northwards in the Kattegat the day before. This vital piece of news was at once sent on to the flagship of the Home Fleet, H.M.S. *King George V*, then in harbour at the main operating base at Scapa Flow in the Orkneys.

When his copy of the Admiralty message was handed to Commander W. J. C. Robertson, the Admiral's Staff Officer (Operations), he instantly realized its urgent significance and at once went along to see the Chief of the Staff, Commodore E. J. P. Brind, who he knew would be waiting for him. On such occasions as these, the Chief of Staff always liked to have a brief talk with Robertson before the two of them went on to the Admiral, so that both could arrange their thoughts to some extent on the immediate situation in readiness for the discussion to come. After a quick verbal survey of the position, lasting two or three minutes, Commodore Brind led the way aft to the Admiral's cabin a few yards away.

Admiral Sir John Tovey, the Commander-in-Chief of the Home Fleet, had already been brought the news of the German

12

warships in the Kattegat by his Secretary, Paymaster-Captain A. W. Paffard. He had immediately put a call through to the Admiralty to gain the latest possible amplifying information from the Director of Naval Intelligence about the reported enemy vessels and to talk over the significance of their appearance with the Vice Chief of the Naval Staff, Vice-Admiral Sir Tom Phillips. It was customary for Sir John to act thus on the receipt of important news, and as the two Staff Officers entered his cabin they were not surprised to see him seated at his desk and talking into the telephone. Such a telephoned conversation between Commander-in-Chief afloat and Admiralty was, of course, only possible as long as the flagship was at its buoy, to which the telephone cable from the shore was led. Over this same line, from this same buoy, Sir David Beatty had spoken to the Admiralty in the previous war and Sir John Jellicoe before him. Once, however, the telephone line was disconnected and the flagship out of harbour, communication with the shore would be greatly restricted, since it would then be confined to the medium of wireless telegraphy, the use of which it was generally desirable to avoid as much as possible, on account of its liability to give away the ship's position to the enemy and of the possibility that the wirelessed messages might be deciphered by him.

When he had finished speaking, Sir John Tovey got up and began to discuss the situation with the two waiting officers. The information that had just come in was obviously of major importance, though not such as to cause surprise. It was, indeed, for just such an eventuality as this that Admiral Tovey's fleet existed and had been stationed in the Orkneys; namely, the appearance of enemy warships in the North Sea. None the less, the report now to hand raised problems that were as difficult as they were pressing. Though enemy war vessels might now be on their way to commence active operations in the area for which the Home Fleet was responsible, it could not be known what those operations were to be: and the possible variation was wide.

The two questions that immediately arose were: what were

these enemy ships that had been seen coming north; and what were they going to do? As to the first question, the thought that almost inevitably came into mind was that one of the German ships might be the *Bismarck*. Sir John Tovey and his staff officers were well aware of the previous intelligence reports of the *Bismarck's* completion and 'working up' in the Baltic. It was, therefore, quite possible that she was one of the two ships seen the day before. If so, the other ship with her might or might not be a capital ship. Probably not. So far as was known, the *Bismarck's* sister ship, the *Tirpitz*, though completed, was not yet ready for sea; while Germany's only other large armoured ships, the battle cruisers *Scharnhorst* and *Gneisenau*, were now at Brest under observation and frequent bombing by the R.A.F.[1] If it were indeed the *Bismarck* that had been in the Kattegat on the previous day, her consort was most likely to be either a pocket battleship or a *Hipper* class cruiser.

It was, however, largely a matter of conjecture whether the *Bismarck* was one of the German squadron or not. The Director of Naval Intelligence could not assure Admiral Tovey definitely that she was, though he thought she might be. In this uncertainty, the wise assumption to make was the most dangerous one; namely, that the *Bismarck* was one of that squadron. Then, if the British plans were based on her being at sea and it later turned out that this was not so after all, the error would be on the safe side and the situation would be more rather than less secure than if the opposite hypothesis were followed. The former assumption was, in fact, made from the start —that the *Bismarck* was coming out.

Much more difficult was the estimation of the enemy's intentions. To reach any conclusion on this question, the antecedent as well as the present evidence had to be taken into account. There had, in fact, been indications for some days that some enemy operation might be imminent. In the second week of May, an unusual amount of German air reconnaissance had

---

[1] Admiral Raeder reported to Hitler on 18th March that the *Tirpitz* should be ready for transfer to Trondjem to continue combat training by the middle of May. The author has, however, been informed by German officers that she did not actually proceed thither till early in 1942.

been noticed between Jan Mayen Island and Greenland; that is, over the sea approaches to Iceland from both east and west.[1] The implications were that the Germans might be making preparations to pass a ship or ships either out into the Atlantic or inwards back to Germany. As there was also a noticeable increase in enemy aerial reconnaissance over Scapa, a circumstance which usually presaged a German naval enterprise of some kind, Sir John Tovey, with the possibility of an enemy movement ever in the forefront of his mind, had signalled to the cruiser *Suffolk*, then on patrol in the Denmark Strait to the north of Iceland, to keep a special watch on the passages in both directions. Next day, as a further precaution, the *Norfolk*, with the Rear-Admiral Commanding the 1st Cruiser Squadron (Rear-Admiral W. F. Wake-Walker) on board, sailed from the war base at Hvalfiord in Iceland to take the *Suffolk's* place so that the latter could return and refuel in readiness for anything that might be impending.

In addition to these indications of possible naval activity by the enemy, there had been persistent rumours over several weeks of troop movements in Norway towards Kirkenes, on the coast well to the north. These rumours Admiral Tovey had interpreted as a possible indication of a coming invasion of or raid on Iceland or the Faroes. Communications across Iceland being very bad, a German force established on the far side of the mountains from the British occupied area might be unapproachable by land, and could probably be fed, supplied and reinforced by air, if not by sea, while its own aircraft would provide a measure of defence against seaborne attack. There had, indeed, been an actual alarm of an airborne invasion of Iceland taking place, though it had turned out to be a false one.

A German foothold in Iceland or capture of the Faroes would mean an intensification of the threat to our Atlantic shipping, the situation in regard to which was already bad enough. To remove our Atlantic convoys as far away as possible from the attentions of the German U-boats and aircraft working from western France, they were being routed a long way to the north

[1] See Diagram 1.

and were passing not far from Iceland itself, from the harbours of which escorting warships and aircraft could conveniently and economically go out to their protection. The nearest enemy air bases on the Norwegian coast were at least 600 miles to the eastward, and therefore too far for effective use against the Allied shipping in the Iceland area. But if these bases were advanced to the Faroes or to Iceland itself, it would be a different matter; and the whole value of the northward diversion of shipping away from the French ports seriously jeopardized. In addition, the British bases at Reykjavik and Hvalfiord in Iceland would be brought under German air attack, possibly be made unusable, and thus the work of the U-boats and the passage of German surface raiders into the Atlantic greatly facilitated.

On the other hand, since the British held the command of the sea, a German seizure of the Faroes or a portion of Iceland could be but temporary, and the German garrison would be ejected in due course. But the organization for doing so was still in a comparatively undeveloped state, the recapture would take time, and during that time much additional destruction of shipping might be done.

In view of this previous intelligence, the report that eleven merchant ships were in company with the German warships when in the Kattegat on May 20th was clearly a factor of potential importance. Ruling out the improbable hypothesis that the proximity of convoy and large warships was entirely accidental, it could be assumed that the latter were acting as the convoy's big-ship escort. And if so, the possible nature and destination of the convoy might give a clue to the movements of the warships accompanying it.

There might, for instance, be a military force already on board the ships of the convoy intended for an immediate descent on Iceland or the Faroes. Or the convoy might have no troops on board at present but be picking up a military raiding force at Kirkenes or elsewhere in Norway, to be followed by a quick dash across to the objective. In either case, the German warships would probably be covering the passage of the expedition all the way to Iceland or wherever it might be going, whether the expeditionary force was already afloat or was to be embarked later.

Other possibilities were that the merchant vessels of the convoy were supply ships to attend on the German warships while operating from northern Norwegian bases; or that they had no naval significance at all but were simply military supply ships taking stores or reinforcements to the German garrison in northern Norway. If the latter were the case and the convoy's contents were important enough, it was conceivable that the warship escort had been specially provided for the purpose of protecting the convoy over the dangerous sea passage along the south Norwegian coast. Once the convoy had reached Bergen, it would be able to proceed further north, assuming it was going further north, through the 'inner leads' or channels between the numerous islands off the coast and the adjacent mainland, and would there be sufficiently secure from attack to need no escort. In that case, the two big warships might be returning to Germany after dropping the convoy at Bergen. Or, on the assumption that the warships had been sailing anyway on some separate project of their own, the opportunity might have been embraced to let them take a convoy with them as far as Bergen, before they went on by themselves. And if the warships were going on by themselves, it could hardly mean other than that they intended to break out into the Atlantic.

The list of possibilities therefore came to this:

(*a*) The enemy warships might be escorting the convoy to Norway as a primary duty, afterwards returning to Germany.

(*b*) They might be escorting the convoy northward for their own use when operating from the Norwegian coast.

(*c*) They might be escorting the convoy northward preparatory to a military descent on the Faroes or Iceland, for which they were intended to provide the surface cover.

(*d*) They might be escorting the convoy as an incidental duty, and afterwards be breaking out into the Atlantic.

The question was, which of these four possible courses of action would the enemy follow? There was really no means of knowing. All were quite if not equally possible, and the only pointer in favour of any particular one was an Admiralty Intelli-

B   17

gence opinion, based on special information, that the ships were about to break out into the Atlantic.

Rather than attempt to make a guess, when there was little or no evidence to give any guidance as to which enemy course of action was the true one, Admiral Tovey considered that the sounder procedure would be to argue out which was the most immediately dangerous enemy course of action and prepare against that. Discussion soon made clear the order of priority. Course of action (*a*) was obviously the least dangerous. Course (*b*) implied a less definite and slightly more remote danger than course (*d*). Course (*c*) might have, if successful, as serious ultimate strategical results and possibly greater political effect than course (*d*). But course (*c*) would take longer to develop and carry through. The Admiral's final decision therefore was that an Atlantic break-out was the enemy course of action that constituted the greatest immediate menace and hence was the one on which he would base his plans. Moreover, the dispositions he might adopt for meeting that contingency should not be incompatible with dealing also with an attempted landing in Iceland or the Faroes.

This crucial point being settled, the next step was to consider what route the enemy might take in breaking out. There were five passages by which he could go. There was the Denmark Strait between Iceland and the east coast of Greenland. There was the passage immediately south of Iceland, between it and the Faroes. There was the passage between the Faroes and the Shetlands. There was the Fair Island channel between the Shetlands and the Orkneys; and, lastly, there was the Pentland Firth. The Pentland Firth could safely be ruled out; but all the other four were possible.

The Fair Island channel is about sixty miles wide. The channel between the Shetlands and the Faroes is 150 miles: that between the Faroes and Iceland 240 miles. The Denmark Strait, though geographically about 200 miles wide, is narrowed to varying degrees by the ice pack which extends many miles south-east from the coast of Greenland. At this time, the clear channel between the edge of the ice and Iceland was only about sixty miles wide. An artificial constriction had also been made at the

18

north-eastern end of the Denmark Strait by the placing of mine-
fields running out for about fifty miles from the northern coast
of Iceland.[1]

The selection of which of these four routes the enemy was
most likely to take was far from obvious. The Faroes-Iceland
passage was wider than the Faroes-Shetlands passage, but the
latter was quite wide enough for escape purposes. The Fair
Island channel was much narrower than either and was the
closest to the British main base. It was not a very likely exit but
it was a just possible one. The Denmark Strait was also narrow.
On the other hand, it was frequently shrouded in fogs and snow
squalls, favourable to an unseen break-out.

The nearer the escape route to the British Isles, the easier it
could be watched by naval and air patrols; but the greater also
the chance of the Germans getting a clear lead on their pursuers.
The Denmark Strait, for all its mistiness, meant a very long
northerly detour for the Germans before the Atlantic proper
was reached, and would leave any British intercepting ships with
the maximum of advantage in the way of interior lines, provided
—but only provided—the escapers could be picked up and
shadowed while traversing the Strait.

One piece of evidence that pointed towards the Denmark
Strait was the belief in Admiralty Intelligence circles that all
previous German naval escapes had been by that route. But even
if this were true, there could be no guarantee that the enemy
would not break the sequence on this occasion.

After a careful discussion of the pros and cons, Sir John
Tovey decided that there was a margin of probability in favour
of the Denmark Strait, but that, even so, the other three more
southerly passages could not be neglected.

The next question was what dispositions to make to watch
the exits.

[1] See Diagram 3.

CHAPTER 2

The Home Fleet Begins to Move

The ships of his command which Sir John Tovey had available for immediate operations were :[1]

Battleships	*King George V* (flagship)
	Prince of Wales
Battle Cruiser	*Hood* (flagship)
8-in. gun Cruisers	*Norfolk* (flagship)
	Suffolk
6-in. gun Cruisers	*Galatea* (flagship)
	Aurora
	Kenya
	Hermione
	Neptune
	Birmingham
	Manchester
	Arethusa
Destroyers	*Electra*
	Anthony
	Echo
	Icarus
	Achates
	Antelope
	Active
	Punjabi
	Nestor

[1] For a list of Flag and Commanding Officers see Appendix I.

May 21st

Destroyers   *Inglefield*
                           Intrepid
                           Lance

Of these, all were with him in harbour at Scapa Flow except the following:

Norfolk was on patrol in the Denmark Strait.

Suffolk was in Hvalfiord, Iceland, refuelling.

Birmingham and *Manchester* were on patrol in the Iceland-Faroes passage.

Arethusa had been taking the Vice-Admiral, Orkneys and Shetlands, on a visit of inspection to Iceland and was due at Reykjavik with him that day.

Hermione was on the way to Scapa after repairs to one of her turrets, being due to arrive on the 22nd.

Inglefield and *Intrepid* were on passage to Scapa from the south and were also due to arrive on the 22nd.

There was also at Scapa the aircraft carrier *Victorious*. She was not, however, part of the Home Fleet, but was under orders to provide the air escort for the important troop convoy WS8B, due to sail for Gibraltar from the Clyde on the 22nd. *Victorious* had only gone to Scapa to embark aircraft preparatory to this convoy duty.

Another big ship detailed to accompany the same convoy was the battle cruiser *Repulse*, who was already at the Clyde in readiness to sail.

When the news of the *Bismarck's* possible sailing reached the Admiralty, it was not long before it was realized that Sir John Tovey could do with some reinforcement. For such an occasion as this a plain comparison of forces did not necessarily give a true measure of requirements. The enemy had the initiative and the British were initially confronted with search and chase problems which might well prove of some complexity. Such operations were notoriously expensive of ships; and early in the forenoon the Vice-Chief of the Naval Staff was telling Sir John Tovey by telephone that the *Victorious* and *Repulse* were being put at

21

his disposal and that the latter had been told to sail north from the Clyde to join his flag.

This gave Sir John Tovey a force of two battleships (*King George V* and *Prince of Wales*), two battle cruisers (*Hood* and *Repulse*), and one aircraft carrier (*Victorious*) to give battle to the *Bismarck*, if it were she who was about to break out. These odds of four or five ships to one, or of two separate battle forces of at least two ships to one, look satisfactory enough at first glance. They need, however, a certain amount of qualification. The *Bismarck* was undoubtedly a tough proposition. She was brand new. She was probably larger than any British battleship, and was believed to have about six feet greater beam, a feature which was specially valuable in conferring superior stability and defensive qualities. She carried a main armament of eight 15-in. guns, 1-in. larger in calibre than those of the latest British battleships, and was believed to be as fast as or faster than any British capital ship afloat. Moreover, the Germans had demonstrated in the previous war their ability to build exceptionally strong warships, able to stand greater punishment than their British counterparts. In addition, there was reason to think that the *Bismarck* had been given plenty of time in the comparatively secure waters of the Baltic for target practice, exercises, and the training of the ship's company, and that she was by now a thoroughly efficient fighting unit.

All the British big ships by no means presented a similar high quality. The *Repulse* was twenty-five years old and had two guns less than the *Bismarck*. Moreover, she was very weakly armoured, and of short fuel endurance.

The *Prince of Wales*, conversely, was too new. She had joined the fleet less than two months before, and with many of the contractor's workmen still on board. Two of her turrets were not actually handed over to the Navy by the firm until April 27th, hardly more than three weeks before, and not till then could training with the whole armament be started. Captain Leach had therefore had quite insufficient time to work his ship's company up to battle efficiency and to 'run in' the machinery. When Admiral Jellicoe commanded the Grand Fleet from 1914 to

1916, he would not take a new ship to sea with the fleet till she had had two months' full training at the fleet base.[1]

The *Victorious* was in much the same condition as the *Prince of Wales*. She had first commissioned at the builders' yard at Newcastle-on-Tyne two months before and had gone straight to the naval dockyard at Rosyth to dock. There she remained till May 16th, when she proceeded to Scapa to complete her trials and to embark two squadrons of aircraft in readiness for her forthcoming convoy trip to the Mediterranean. The outstanding trials and the essential tuning-in of wireless and radar installations had been completed by the evening of May 20th, and on the morning of the 21st—the day with which we are now dealing—*Victorious* had gone to sea to embark her aircraft. When Sir John Tovey was being informed that she was now at his disposal, she was outside the harbour and was engaged in flying on nine Swordfish aircraft of No. 825 Squadron and six Fulmars of No. 800Z Squadron. The Swordfish squadron had been well trained and worked up under its leader, Lieutenant-Commander E. Esmonde. Moreover, two or three of the aircraft were equipped with some of the first A.S.V. radar sets and had had opportunities to practise with them. But the squadron was intended for combined operations work and had not therefore carried out its deck-landing training. None of the 'hostilities only' pilots had, in fact, ever before landed on a carrier's deck. The Fulmars were not a squadron in the true sense, as they were manned by a scratch lot of pilots and observers who had been got together for the trip to the Mediterranean only, and the observers especially were short of training of every kind.

As soon as the aircraft were on board, deck-landing training was started. But only two or three pilots were able to do practice landings before the ship returned to harbour for the night. In respect, therefore, both of herself and her aircraft, *Victorious* was anything but a fully efficient unit.

---

[1] Though since the Grand Fleet battleships numbered more than thirty, one ship more or less made far less difference to Admiral Jellicoe than it did to Admiral Tovey.

The Home Fleet Begins to Move

Of the remaining two heavy ships, *King George V* and *Hood*, the latter was over twenty years old; and during those years there had been a number of improvements in warship design from which the *Hood* had naturally not benefited. If somewhat outmoded, however, she was nevertheless a powerful unit with a main armament as strong as that of the *Bismarck*. Thus, of Admiral Tovey's five large ships, two (*Prince of Wales* and *Victorious*) were some way from being fully efficient, one (*Repulse*) was considerably weaker than the *Bismarck*, and a fourth (*Hood*) was rather long in the tooth. The Admiral had therefore only one ship (*King George V*) that could at this time properly be regarded as a fair match for such a vessel as the *Bismarck*.

The general picture in the mind of Admiral Tovey after he had been discussing the situation with his staff for some time can now be appreciated. He was assuming that the *Bismarck* was one of the two German ships seen coming north in the Kattegat on May 20th. He had decided that the contingency of her and her consort endeavouring to break out into the Atlantic was the one to be primarily provided against. He had also reached the conclusion that while there was a balance of probability in favour of the Germans using the Denmark Strait escape route, the southerly channels between Iceland and the Faroes and between the Faroes and the Orkneys could not be ignored. Therefore, the interception dispositions should, if possible, be designed to cover all of them; though, in case of shortage, the order of priority should run from north to south. Finally, the formidable nature of the *Bismarck* as a fighting ship he fully recognized; and while the British strength had been increased by the attachment of the *Repulse* and *Victorious* to his command, the weakness of the first and the unpreparedness of the second and also of the *Prince of Wales* were factors to be borne in mind.

It took round about two hours for these provisional conclusions to be reached. The Commander-in-Chief had mainly discussed the matter with the two staff officers already mentioned: but others were sent for from time to time and came in perhaps to answer two or three questions or to make a longer stay. The Admiral's navigating officer, known as the 'Master of the

24

Fleet', was soon there with charts of the North Atlantic and Arctic Seas, to draw pencil circles showing enemy 'farthest on' curves according to which channel he chose, what speed he used, and what time he left harbour to commence his break-out. After considering all the evidence and hearing all opinions, Sir John Tovey roughed out his preliminary dispositions for meeting the emergency. First, as to keeping watch on the exits, he would

(*a*) Send the *Suffolk* to join the *Norfolk* in the Denmark Strait; though in order to conserve fuel, she should not rejoin the patrol until just before the enemy's earliest possible time of arrival in the Strait.

(*b*) Send the *Birmingham* and *Manchester* to refuel at Skaalifjord and then resume their patrol in the Iceland-Faroes channel.

(*c*) Order the *Arethusa* to remain at Hvalfiord at the disposal of the Rear-Admiral commanding the 1st Cruiser Squadron in the *Norfolk*.

(*d*) Ask for air reconnaissance of all passages from Greenland to the Orkneys.

Next as to the interception and destruction of the enemy: the Admiral decided to divide his heavy ships into two forces. One of these, to consist of the *Hood* and *Prince of Wales* under Vice-Admiral L. E. Holland in the *Hood*, he would send north to Iceland to be handy for the Denmark Strait and the Iceland-Faroes passage, which the Commander-in-Chief regarded as the two most likely exits. The other heavy force would consist of his own flagship and the *Victorious*, later to be joined by the *Repulse* from the Clyde. With this force, the Commander-in-Chief would cover the passages from the Faroes southwards.

The question remained when to put these dispositions into force. The Commander-in-Chief had brought all ships at Scapa to short (two hours') notice for steam already. But actually to sail the ships was a different matter, and one which was dominated by the question of fuel expenditure. It was possible that the enemy, if he were bent on escape into the Atlantic, would be caught in one of the exit channels and brought to action near to a British base. But this could not be guaranteed. An Atlantic break-out attempt might very well mean a long chase over many hundreds of miles of ocean; and if so, considerations of fuel supply would certainly play an important and possibly a decisive part in whether the chase was successful. The *Bismarck* would assuredly start with her oil tanks full. If then the British interceptor forces were sailed too early and patrolled fruitlessly for a number of hours while the *Bismarck* was still in harbour, they would be that much short of fuel when she did eventually emerge. On the other hand, if they were delayed sailing too long, she might get out before them, with too long a start to be caught up. The only solution of this harassing dilemma lay in accurate information of the enemy's whereabouts and movements, and both Sir John Tovey and the Admiralty staff had from the first realized the urgent need of obtaining it.

It was mainly the Admiralty's province to arrange for this to be done. The obvious means of reconnaissance of the enemy's position was aerial. The southern part of the Norwegian coast was within comparatively easy flying distance from British airfields, but to search it by aircraft meant obtaining the co-operation of the Royal Air Force. This the Admiralty could do by contacting the Air Ministry direct, leaving it to the Air Staff to give orders to the appropriate air command. Or the Admiralty could ring up the Headquarters Coastal Command, by virtue of its close liaison with that command. Yet a third line of approach was via the naval Commander-in-Chief at Rosyth who had the A.O.C. 18 Group of the R.A.F. Coastal Command at his side and could request searches by the aircraft of one or more of his stations. The initiative in each case, however, lay with the shore authorities and not with the Commander-in-Chief, Home Fleet, though the latter was closely interested in the results of any reconnaissance arranged.

The Admiralty, aware of Sir John Tovey's greedy anxiety for news of the enemy, which indeed they felt just as keenly themselves, took care to keep him informed of what was being done to spy out the Norwegian harbours. They were able to tell him that special Spitfires of the Coastal Command Photographic Reconnaissance Unit would be taking off about 11 a.m. to search the Norwegian coastline. Hearing of this while he was

26

still at grips with the interception problem, Sir John Tovey made up his mind to await the hoped-for information of the enemy ships that might emerge from these reconnaissance flights before despatching his naval forces to their pre-determined stations, and thus beginning the drain on their precious oil fuel supplies.

The Spitfires went as arranged. One of them, piloted by Flying Officer Churchill, searched the Skaggerack and Oslo Fiord, but sighted no warships. Another similar aircraft, piloted by Flying Officer Suckling, was instructed to search the western approaches to the Skaggerack and the Norwegian coast as far north as Bergen. Almost at the end of his search he sighted two warships in the secluded Grimstad Fiord just south of Bergen, and these he photographed. This was at 1.15 p.m. on May 21st.

Suckling landed at Wick airfield at 2.45 p.m. and reported by word of mouth having seen two cruisers. But his personal estimate was incorrect. When his photographs had been developed, they showed to the expert examiners who eagerly scrutinized them that what he had really discovered were a battleship of the *Bismarck* class and a *Hipper* class cruiser. So the *Bismarck* it was.

The exciting evidence contained in Suckling's photographs set activity in train in a number of directions. Arrangements were at once put in hand for attacking the enemy in his now discovered lair. A bombing attack should take place that night by six Whitleys and six Hudsons of Coastal Command, and a strong force of bombers and torpedo-carrying aircraft was ordered to assemble for still stronger attacks after daylight.

Up in the Orkneys, as the *Victorious* came back to harbour in the evening after embarking her aircraft, a signal was seen flying in the flagship for her captain to come over to see the Commander-in-Chief at once. Arriving on board the *King George V*, Captain Bovell was informed by Sir John Tovey that the *Bismarck* was near Bergen and was asked if his aircraft could carry out an attack on her there. He replied that, in his opinion, the slow and out-of-date Swordfish, which could hardly do more than 80 m.p.h., would be very unlikely to do any good against ships in so strongly defended a place as Bergen. The Admiral then asked whether, if the *Bismarck* should manage to get away to sea, the *Victorious* was in a fit state to proceed with the fleet in pursuit of her.

It was fairly obvious to all present that she was, by every reasonable standard, quite unfit. Captain Bovell answered, however, that his own inclination was to say that his ship should go: but that in the circumstances he felt it was desirable to take his experts' advice before giving a firm opinion. He therefore asked if Commander H. C. Ranald, his Commander (Flying), and Lieutenant-Commander Esmonde, his senior squadron leader, could come over for consultation. After arriving in the Admiral's cabin, these two officers backed their Captain up in saying that the *Victorious* should sail with the fleet. He and they then went back to their ship, leaving their Admiral pondering whether it was sensible or right to take so raw a vessel with him on operations against a ship like the *Bismarck*. Very probably it was not. Experienced and capable an officer as Captain Bovell was, he had only received his air crews that day and manifestly could do next to nothing to improve their efficiency in a matter of a few hours. Those air crews had to be accepted as virtually untrained for carrier flying. Their fleet operational value could, therefore, be little more than was represented by the individual characteristics of courage and dash of the flyers themselves. This Sir John Tovey could only estimate by what he had just seen of their senior member and leader, Lieutenant-Commander Esmonde; and it was admittedly a very chancy test. Even, however, in the very short time he had been on board the flagship, Esmonde[1] had made a very favourable impression on the Admiral; and the latter made up his mind, very largely on this evidence, that if he went to sea the *Victorious* should go with him.

The Commander-in-Chief was also coming to the decision that it was time Vice-Admiral Holland's force was sent to sea. By 9 p.m. it was over seven hours since the enemy had first been seen near Bergen, and no further sighting reports had since come through. Moreover, the weather reports were unpromising, and

---

[1] He was afterwards awarded a posthumous V.C. for his part in attacking the *Scharnhorst* and *Gneisenau* during their dash up the Channel.

it might be that no more sightings would be made for some time.[1] It would therefore be a good thing to get the *Hood* and her squadron started on their way north. A signal was consequently made to the Vice-Admiral to proceed with the *Hood, Prince of Wales,* and the destroyers *Electra, Anthony, Echo, Icarus, Achates,* and *Antelope*; and this force left harbour about midnight, with orders to fuel at Hvalfiord and then cover the patrols north of the latitude of 62° North.

The location of the enemy near Bergen was puzzling. Bergen was almost the nearest point of Norway to the British Isles and therefore the easiest to be kept under aerial observation. It was a long way south of Iceland, and an enemy ship contemplating a break-out through the Denmark Strait could surely be expected to find an anchorage farther up the Norwegian coast, such as Trondhjem or Narvik, either of which would have been practically beyond British shore-based air range and at the same time almost as close to the more northerly exit channel. The use of Bergen by the *Bismarck* suggested either that she was not intending an Atlantic dash and therefore did not mind being sighted in a Norwegian harbour, or that she meant to escape by one of the more southerly routes. Sir John Tovey felt that the wisdom of his division of his force was strengthened and that it was very desirable that the Faroes-Orkneys channels should not be left uncovered.

Meanwhile, the flying weather had been steadily deteriorating. Mist and rain had set in over a large part of the North Sea, and when that night the R.A.F. bombers went out for their attacks on the German ships, they found it very difficult to find the Norwegian coast. Only two aircraft did, in fact, manage to discover it, and they could not be sure which part of the coastline it was. These two aimed their bombs at dimly seen shipping which could not properly be identified, and the bombers returned without knowing whether they had scored any hits or, if so, on what.

When day came, the weather was just as bad, if not worse.

---

[1] It is probable that the report of the sighting near Bergen at 1.15 p.m. reached the Commander-in-Chief between 3.30 and 4 p.m.

The Home Fleet Begins to Move

Reconnaissance aircraft sent out to search the Bergen area reported that the conditions were extremely adverse, with cloud down to 200 feet. By 10 a.m. it was being reported that the visibility had shut down completely and that no reconnaissance was possible; and later attempts had no more success. The striking force of bombers and torpedo-aircraft could not therefore be despatched, and remained on the ground.

As the hours passed without news of the enemy and with only dismal reports of bad flying conditions, mounting anxiety began inevitably to be felt in the flagship. By lunch time, twenty-four hours had passed since the enemy had last been seen, and the scope of his possible activities during that long period was becoming alarmingly wide. The ships might still be at anchor near Bergen. But they could also be 500 or 600 miles on their way to another destination, wherever it might be. They could by this time be nearly at Iceland: or, if they had passed to the southward of the island en route for the Atlantic, they could be well past any of the exit channels between Iceland and the Orkneys.

It is not difficult to picture Sir John Tovey's unease of mind in this situation. For all he knew, his enemy might be well out to sea and steaming farther beyond reach with every minute that went by. This possibility naturally made the Admiral want to get to sea and take ground to the westward. Yet if he did so and the enemy had not after all gone out, the British ships would merely be wasting fuel while the enemy was still in harbour with his oil tanks full. Faced with such a choice of evils, Sir John Tovey decided to hang on as long as possible in harbour, where he would at all events be on the telephone to the Admiralty and therefore in a position to receive any fresh word of the enemy by the quickest possible route.

But still no news came through. Air reconnaissance which theoretically should have been able to keep the German ships under more or less constant observation had become impotent through unfavourable weather. Or all but impotent. On the main Orkney island, near to the capital, Kirkwall, was the naval air station of Hatston, under the command of Captain

30

H. L. St. J. Fancourt, R.N. The main purpose of his air station was to train newly formed Fleet Air Arm squadrons prior to their embarkation in a carrier. If the completion of this preliminary training did not happen to coincide with allocation to a ship, there was an arrangement whereby the squadron concerned operated from Hatston on convoy duty under the general direction of the R.A.F. Coastal Command. There was one such squadron at Hatston at this time, No. 828, consisting of Albacore torpedo planes; and when the enemy ships were first sighted, Captain Fancourt rang up the headquarters of Coastal Command and obtained its release from convoy duty preparatory to its use as a striking force against the enemy ships. From Hatston to Bergen was, however, only just within the Albacores' fuel range. The Shetlands were appreciably nearer to Bergen, and so Captain Fancourt determined to move the squadron up to those islands prior to flying them off to the attack. The arrangements for doing so could not, however, be completed on the 21st, and the departure of the squadron was therefore postponed till the 22nd.

The bad weather of the 22nd and the consequent failure of aerial reconnaissance of the enemy's last known position was of direct concern to Captain Fancourt in view of the intended torpedo strike by his Albacores. He was therefore in frequent touch with Coastal Command regarding the fortunes of its reconnaissance aircraft and was well aware of the difficulties they were meeting and of their inability to make the Norwegian coast. Not only did these negative results hold up his own Albacore striking force, but he, as a naval officer, was also conscious of the acute desire that the Commander-in-Chief of the Home Fleet must be feeling for a successful search of the *Bismarck's* last reported anchorage near Bergen.

As it became increasingly clear to him, therefore, that the R.A.F. reconnaissance was unlikely to achieve a look into the crucial fiord, Captain Fancourt began to cast about in his mind as to whether he himself could do something to gain the urgently required information. It occured to him that he had one or two Fleet Air Arm officers in his command with many years' experience of flying over the sea in all sorts of weather and that a really first-class crew of this kind might have a very fair chance of reaching Bergen, even in the filthy weather then prevailing. Indeed, provided the navigation could be accurately done, the present low visibility was actually an advantage, since it would give promise of an unseen approach to Bergen and therefore of protection against the strong German fighter force stationed there.

Following this line of thought, Captain Fancourt mentally picked on Commander G. A. Rotherham as the man most likely to bring off the required feat. Commander Rotherham was actually at Hatston for administrative duties and normally did no flying. But he was a Fleet Air Arm observer of long experience, which covered the earlier and more rudimentary days of naval flying when aids to navigation by means of instruments and wireless beams were none too well developed, in default of which the naval flying personnel was accustomed to rely considerably on rough-and-ready methods, such as close observation of wave appearance on the surface of the sea, in judging the strength and direction of the wind and hence the right course to steer. By such means they had often 'smelt' their way back to their carriers when scientific aids were absent or had failed them. For the purpose of a flight to Bergen, such experience of a 'bow and arrow' character might be invaluable in dealing with the low cloud conditions to be contended with.

Then there was the question of what aircraft to use. The Albacores had already gone to the Shetlands. But there were at Hatston two long-range American twin-engined Maryland bombers, the normal use of which was as height-finding and target-towing aircraft for training with the fleet in Scapa. They were not operationally equipped, except that their gun armament was mounted, and up-to-date navigational appliances were lacking. It was, however, one of these machines or nothing.

Accordingly, somewhere about 2 p.m., Captain Fancourt asked Coastal Command, to whose orders he was subject, if there was any objection to the proposed flight. Receiving immediate approval, he rang up the flagship and likewise received the Commander-in-Chief's blessing to the project. Captain Fan-

1. The German battleship *Bismarck*. Armament: eight 15-in. and twelve 5·9-in., guns plus many anti-aircraft weapons

2. The *Bismarck* discovered near Bergen by an R.A.F. photograph

3. Sir John Tovey, Commander-in-Chief, Home Fleet

court then sent for Commander Rotherham and propounded to him the idea of a flight to Bergen. Rotherham immediately expressed his readiness to make the attempt. A pilot had also to be selected. But this problem solved itself; for when the news got round the station that a Maryland was going, the officer in command of the target-towing squadron, Lieutenant-Commander Goddard, declared roundly that no one other than himself would pilot the machine; and, from numerous volunteers, the wireless operator and rear-gunner, Armstrong and Milne, were selected. Thus the crew was quickly made up.

It was not just a matter of jumping into a plane and roaring away. A flight of this difficulty and importance had to be very carefully prepared. Where navigation was likely to be mainly a matter of dead reckoning and shore identification very questionable, Rotherham decided to adopt the old naval device of steering for a point some miles to the right or left of the real destination with a view to knowing which way to turn if a doubtful landfall were made. In this case, he selected an island about fifteen miles to the right of his real objective, with the intention of turning left along the coast when land was seen—if indeed it was seen at all before he hit it. Several hours were spent in making calculations, examining and endeavouring to memorize photographs of the Norwegian coast, and gaining what intelligence was available. Coastal Command Headquarters were consulted and advised an approach at 200 feet with the object of defeating the enemy's radar and so avoiding the early attention of his fighters, which were said to be in great strength.

At about 4.30 p.m., when the failure of another attempt by R.A.F. aircraft to reach Bergen came through, the Maryland took off. The weather at first was clear but soon deteriorated, after which the journey across can be described as a succession of ducks and drakes. When they ran into mist, they began to fly within sight of the surface so as to keep an eye on windage. But the cloud got so low that they came to be almost skimming the surface, and the pilot, who had a more restricted view than Rotherham, found the strain such that he went up to 3,000 feet. After flying some time at this height, Rotherham decided he must see the surface again, and down they went into the cloud. The sea came in sight dangerously close, and the pilot had so much difficulty in not flying into it that after a little he said he must again go up. They had, however, obtained a valuable glimpse of the water, which enabled a new estimation of the strength and direction of the wind to be made. Again they went up above cloud level, and again after a while they came down for another surface skim, followed by yet another climb. After a breather up high Rotherham reckoned they were within ten minutes of their landfall, and that a further descent was imperative. They were nerving themselves for the possibility of flying straight into a hillside when Providence decided to show favour to temerity. At this critical moment, the clouds began to break, and right ahead they saw the very island for which they had been making.

Navigationally, the worst difficulties were over. In fair visibility, they flew left up the coast and soon found the fiord where the German ships had been lying. It was quite empty, but to make sure they circled round again, and then made for Bergen to examine the harbour there. About this time the 'inter-comm' decided to go out of action. As they passed over the town, the defence opened up with every gun. Commander Rotherham wanted to climb into the clouds to get cover but could not communicate with the pilot, who took the opposite view and proceeded to dive. Down through a hurricane of projectiles they tore until they were roaring over Bergen at only about 200 feet from the house tops. Then out to sea, astonished that they were still intact.

Commander Rotherham realized the vital importance of signalling the information that the German ships had sailed as quickly as possible, lest he be shot down by German fighters before it went off. Unable to telephone, he wrote a message to the Commander-in-Chief that 'the battleship and cruiser have left', and pushed it up through a hole to the pilot, who passed it to the wireless operator. The latter spent some time calling up Coastal Command to whose wave he was tuned, but without result. Realizing that there might be some maladjustment on this unaccustomed wave, he proceeded on his own initiative to change to his normal target-towing wave at Scapa and passed the message on that. At Scapa, target-towing was actually taking place and the accompanying wireless traffic was in progress when, to their great surprise, the operators took in a most urgent operational signal. This was at about 7 p.m. The Maryland flew on to Sumbrugh in the Shetlands, whither Captain Fancourt had now followed up his Albacores, and landed at about 7.45 p.m.

Commander Rotherham had hardly climbed out of his aircraft when he was told he was wanted on the Orkneys telephone. There he found himself speaking to the Admiral's Chief of Staff. The signal sent off about the enemy ships having left had reached the flagship, but the Admiral had decided that as such important issues depended on what Commander Rotherham had seen, it would be worth while to wait the extra half-hour or so till he had landed and could be interrogated personally. The Admiral and his staff were just sitting down to dinner when Commodore Brind came in with the report of Rotherham's telephoned conversation. It satisfied the Admiral that the enemy had really left the Bergen area. He therefore gave orders for the fleet in Scapa to be ready to weigh at 10 p.m., the earliest time steam could be ready. He also sent out three signals to the northern forces, these telling:

(*a*) The *Suffolk* to return to the Denmark Strait to join the *Norfolk*.

(*b*) The *Arethusa* to join the *Manchester* and *Birmingham* in the Iceland-Faroes passage.

(*c*) The Vice-Admiral in the *Hood*, then on passage with his force to Hvalfiord, to proceed instead as necessary to cover the Iceland-Faroes passage and the Denmark Strait.

At 10.15 p.m., the fleet in Scapa was aweigh and the leading ships were making for the gates. By 11 p.m. all ships were in the Pentland Firth and steaming westward towards the Atlantic.

CHAPTER 3

All-night Shadowing and
a Dawn Battle

D uring the night hours, the Commander-in-Chief's
squadron was passing along the north coast of Scotland. About 7 a.m., when they were abreast the Butt of
Lewis, the *Repulse* accompanied by three destroyers was sighted
coming up from the Clyde, and she formed in astern of the flagship. Daylight had come to show cheerless weather, rainclouds
covering the sky, with a cold wind and moderate sea from the
north-west, almost ahead. The outlook for air reconnaissance
was obviously poor.

Having made his junction with the *Repulse*, the Commander-
in-Chief altered course to north-west to reach a good position
for covering the exits south of the Faroes. For hour after hour
the fleet plugged along against the seas without any news of the
enemy. Noon passed and 2 p.m. At 3 p.m. the Admiral had got
as far northward as he wanted and he turned westward in the
direction of enemy escape. But when the men off watch went to
tea at 4 p.m., there was still no word. Six o'clock went by and
eight o'clock. Twenty-four hours had now passed since the
Admiral had received Commander Rotherham's message that
the enemy ships had left their Bergen fiord, and Sir John Tovey
would not have denied that he had begun to feel concerned
about the continued silence from all his patrolling forces. Lean-
ing over the chart with Commodore Brind and looking again,
as he had done frequently before that day, at the distance curves
from Bergen drawn for every so many hundred miles, he re-

flected how very wide was the margin of uncertainty in his en-
deavours to locate the enemy ships. They could have left the
Bergen area anything between fifty-four and twenty-four hours
before, a difference of thirty whole hours during which they could
have covered a good 700 miles without excessive haste; and
so large a possible variation was more than anyone could
cater for. The cruisers ordered to watch the Iceland-Faroes passage should have got back to their patrol lines just in time after
refuelling in Iceland. But each had about eighty miles of line
to watch and their circle of visibility was probably no more
than twenty miles in diameter. There was therefore a good
chance of a patrol-runner getting through the look-out line unseen. Radar would help a little but not a great deal, since in
its then state of development its surface range was below that
of ordinary eyesight on a fine day.

Air searches, had they been in full operation, might have made
a lot of difference. But the weather was against them. Before
leaving harbour the night before, Sir John Tovey had asked for
air patrols on the following day to cover the Denmark Strait, the
Iceland-Faroes passage, the Faroes-Shetland passage, and the
Norwegian coast. Of these, the Norwegian coast patrol could
not be flown at all, nor that in the Denmark Strait. Sunderlands
of 201 Squadron flew the Iceland-Faroes patrol from early
morning till after 9 p.m., but the Faroes-Shetland patrol had to
be abandoned before 1 p.m., and the back-up patrol to the westward was only in operation from 1 p.m. to 5 p.m. Sir John
Tovey was made acquainted with these various failures of the
air reconnaissance,[1] and was therefore well aware of the gaps in
the line of observation through which the enemy ships could
have slipped undiscovered. If they were really making for the
Atlantic, they could easily have reached the chosen exit channel
by now, and the fact that they had not yet been reported might
well mean that they had got through.

Moreover, the original assumption on which the British
fleet movements were based, that the *Bismarck* was bound

[1] Though he did not know at this time that the Denmark Strait air patrol was
not in operation.

for the Atlantic trade routes, might after all have been a false one, and the Admiral might hear at any moment that she was covering a landing in the Faroes or elsewhere while he himself was miles away to the westward. It was a disagreeable thought, even though the Admiral knew that his line of action had been substantially the right one. The complete lack of news all day had, in fact, been somewhat trying. But though Sir John could not know it, the period of initial suspense was nearly over.

An hour earlier, at 7 p.m., Captain R. M. Ellis was standing on the bridge of his cruiser, H.M.S. *Suffolk*, in the Denmark Strait. The bridge had been 'arcticized', which meant that it was closed in and fitted with steam heating, and was therefore tolerably warm. Captain Ellis had been on the bridge all that day and all the night before, and indeed the night before that. His ship had recently been on patrol for ten days and had been recalled to refuel two days before. That had involved a night coastal passage at high speed to Hvalfiord and another night passage back twenty-four hours later after fuelling.

The *Bismarck's* appearance on the Norwegian coast was already known, and on the *Suffolk's* return to the entrance to the Denmark Strait, she was summoned into Isa Fiord to receive final patrol orders from the Flag Officer of the squadron, Rear-Admiral W. F. Wake-Walker, who was in there in his flagship, H.M.S. *Norfolk*, paying a flying visit to the new radar station ashore. The instructions he signalled to Captain Ellis were that the *Suffolk* was to investigate the ice near the top of the mine-fields and then patrol north-east and south-west along the edge of the ice. This was the pack ice that ran out a hundred miles or more from the coast of Greenland towards Iceland. Its extent varied greatly according to the time of year and even from week to week. At this particular time, it covered about half the sea area between Greenland and Iceland, leaving a channel of open water about sixty miles wide between its edge and the Icelandic coast.

The minefields referred to by the Rear-Admiral extended north-west from a point close in to the North Cape of Iceland for about forty miles or so.[1] The Germans knew of these mine-fields, because we had previously published the fact of our having laid minefields thereabouts, though not, of course, their precise extent. The German Naval Staff could, however, make a fair guess from the charted variations in the depth of water how far north-west the outer minefield ran. There was a fair presumption, therefore, that if the *Bismarck* and her consort meant to escape by the Denmark Strait they would pass round the supposed top of this minefield, between it and the ice.

The *Suffolk* had been up to the top of the minefield and had begun her south-west and north-east patrol along the ice. Both *Suffolk* and *Norfolk* had had many months' experience of patrol-ling in the Denmark Strait and were well familiar with its peculiar and generally savage characteristics. In winter, the bitter cold, the prolonged heavy gales, snowstorms, and almost continuous darkness imposed a severe strain on the ships' companies. Even in summer, it was a desolate enough area, though it had a certain rather weird fascination of its own. There was a grim beauty about the lonely and jagged north-west coast of Iceland, white-streaked with the remnants of the winter snow-fields; while on the other side of the Strait, the far-away peaks of Greenland's 'icy mountains' could now and then be seen in distant serration beyond the intervening waste of the shifting pack ice, sometimes glowing a magical pink in the rays of the sunset. The freezing isolation of the Strait, the bitter ferocity of its weather, and the queer mirage effects frequently experienced induced a subconscious sympathy with the Norse legends of giants and goblins inhabiting these forbidding regions.

On the day of which we are now speaking, the weather con-ditions in the Denmark Strait were somewhat unusual. Over the ice it was clear and also for about three miles to the south-east-ward of the ice-edge. The rest of the Strait, almost up to the coast of Iceland, was covered in fog and mist. There was thus a lane of clear water about three miles broad between the ice and the ragged wall of mist which ran out of sight in both directions roughly parallel to the ice.

[1] See Diagram 3.

All-Night Shadowing and a Dawn Battle

Captain Ellis was steaming close in to the ice when on the north-easterly leg of his patrol. But when he had to turn round for the south-westerly run, he made a point of moving over away from the ice to hug the mist. His reason for doing so was this. When proceeding north-east he had an uninterrupted ahead view in the direction from which the *Bismarck* was likely to appear, and could hope to spot her a good way off. But when he was going south-west, the view from the compass platform towards her probable line of approach was interfered with by the bridge structure; besides which the radar was also 'blind' on the sternmost sector. There was therefore appreciably less chance of the *Bismarck*, were she to appear, being readily sighted on an after bearing, when the *Suffolk* was steering south-west, than when the latter was going north-east. Hence, Captain Ellis wanted, when his ship was on the more dangerous south-westerly leg, to have the mist close at hand to slip into quickly if he came unexpectedly under fire.

For it was not the *Suffolk's* business to fight the *Bismarck*. On the contrary, it was her duty to avoid an action with so superior an enemy. Her function was to find and then shadow the *Bismarck*, reporting her position at intervals so that British heavy ships could come up and do the fighting. And to shadow properly, it was essential that the *Suffolk* should avoid being damaged. It was more important that she should retain her speed, manœuvring power, and wireless signalling equipment intact than endeavour to damage the enemy herself. Indeed, it was extremely likely that, if it came to an action, the *Bismarck* would sink her out of hand and would then steam on unharmed and unwatched.[1] Hence Captain Ellis's periodic partiality for the fog-bank that day.

A dive into the fog would, of course, mean losing sight of the *Bismarck* as well as gaining protection from her broadsides. Would that not mean jeopardizing the *Suffolk's* main duty of keeping touch with the enemy? A year before the answer would have been yes. But not now. The radar system of discovering the proximity of ships or other solid objects invisible by reason of

---

[1] The *Suffolk* had had her torpedoes removed during a previous refit.

40

mist or darkness to ordinary eyesight was just being developed in the Navy. The *Suffolk* had very recently been fitted with a new and improved gunnery set with nearly all-round training, the only blank sector being across the stern. Therefore, provided he were able to keep within radar range of the *Bismarck*, Captain Ellis could hope to keep track of her even though the two ships might not be in sight of each other, through one or the other or both being hidden in fog, snowstorms or rain squalls.

The *Suffolk's* sister ship, *Norfolk*, commanded by Captain A. J. L. Phillips, was not nearly so well off in this respect. Her radar set, of an earlier type, was a fixed one which could not be trained round, and was only effective over a small arc of bearing each side of right ahead. On most of the circle of bearing it was inoperative. For detection and shadowing purposes, therefore, the Norfolk's radar was of very small value and was in no way to be compared with the *Suffolk's*.

Captain Ellis felt the more sanguine of his ability to shadow by radar from the fact that he had from the first been personally interested in and had made a special study of the new device. He had instinctively appreciated its possibilities and had lost no opportunity to practise with it when other ships came near enough. The trouble he had taken to instruct himself in the subject was to have a noteworthy reward.

When Rear-Admiral Wake-Walker had given the *Suffolk* her patrol orders earlier in the day, he had said that, unless the weather conditions altered, the *Norfolk* would patrol in the mist about fifteen miles to the southward of *Suffolk*; and Captain Phillips had taken up that position during the afternoon. These were the only two British ships in the Denmark Strait; but, as already described, there were other vessels farther south guarding the Iceland-Faroes channel. There was also a small amount of British air reconnaissance; but, again as previously mentioned, the weather was most unfavourable to flying and only a few of the intended searches were being flown. Among others, the Denmark Strait air patrols had had to be cancelled: so that the *Norfolk* and *Suffolk* on this day knew that they could expect no assistance from the air.

All-Night Shadowing and a Dawn Battle

At 7 p.m., the *Suffolk* was steering south-westward close to the mist, with her stern to the direction of most likely enemy approach. In consequence of the radar being blind on that sector and the view from the compass platform much obstructed, Captain Ellis had had the seamen look-outs strengthened for the after bearings. At 7.22 p.m., there came a hail from the starboard after look-out, Able Seaman Newell, of 'Ship bearing Green 140 (degrees)', quickly corrected to 'two ships' on the same bearing. The Captain and most of those on the compass platform rushed over to that side of the bridge and saw through their binoculars what was undoubtedly the *Bismarck* and a cruiser with her.

They were no more than about 14,000 yards away, a dangerously close range to enemy guns that could shoot up to 40,000 yards. Captain Ellis put his wheel over on the instant to make for the fog, and it was with a feeling of relief that he saw the mist close round his ship. But it had taken him two or three minutes to reach it and he thought it extraordinary that the *Bismarck* had apparently failed to notice him during that time. As he turned, Captain Ellis ordered an enemy report signal to be sent out.

His retreat into the mist took him into the angular space between two of the minefields; and in that space he manœuvred, keeping radar contact all the time, to allow the *Bismarck* to pass him so that he could take up a shadowing position behind her. Watching intently the white dots on the radar screen which represented the two enemy ships, he saw them cross to the northward and move on beyond him. When he thought they were about the right distance away, he steered back into the open. But he found he had misjudged it. The enemy was still too close and he went back into the mist to drop back further. At his second emergence, the enemy ships were about fifteen miles ahead, steering along and close to the ice edge. This distance approximated to what Captain Ellis wanted, and he set course to shadow, sending out a string of wireless signals as he went. The enemy, he soon found, was steaming fast; at from 28 to 30 knots.

Deep in the mist, the *Norfolk* took in those signals. The Captain's dinner had been brought up to his sea cabin and he was munching some welsh rarebit when the Chief Yeoman of Signals almost fell through the door with the excited announcement: '*Suffolk's* got 'em, sir,' and handed him the enemy report. Captain Phillips was on the compass platform in a moment to order the course to be altered to close the enemy's reported position at high speed. The ship went to action stations and a number of depth charges on the upper deck were jettisoned. At 8.30 p.m., after an hour's hard steaming, the *Norfolk* suddenly ran out of the mist and sighted the *Bismarck* and her attendant cruiser (later known to be the *Prinz Eugen*) on the port bow on a nearly opposite course and at an estimated range of six miles. The two sides were closing rapidly and the *Norfolk's* position was highly critical. Captain Phillips put the wheel hard-a-starboard to get back into the mist and made smoke to cover his withdrawal. This time the *Bismarck* was on the alert and opened a very accurate fire. Three 15-in. salvoes straddled the *Norfolk* and another came down in her wake. By immense good fortune she was not hit. Some large splinters came on board, but she got back into the mist undamaged.

She, too, made an enemy report: and it happened that this gave the first news to the Commander-in-Chief and the Admiralty that the *Bismarck* had been discovered. That the *Suffolk's* reports had not been taken in may have been due to her recent long patrol in fog and mist, making the aerial trunking sodden with moisture without any transmitting to dry the leads out. Later, after a number of enemy reports, the *Suffolk's* transmission became normal.

After the *Norfolk* had obtained sanctuary in the mist she, like the *Suffolk* a little earlier, manœuvred to take station well behind the enemy. For her, however, it was a more difficult calculation, since without a training radar set she lost all touch with the enemy ships when she entered the mist. Captain Phillips had therefore to rely entirely on guesswork in judging when to turn on to the shadowing course. He also had to decide what this course was to be. The *Suffolk*, he knew, was in the clear channel between the mist and the ice, and he could tell from her reports that she was more or less right astern of the enemy, who clearly could not escape to starboard on account of the ice. There was, however, open water on the enemy's port side. The obvious post for the *Norfolk*, therefore, was out on the enemy's port quarter, ready for a turn by him in that direction. But to remain on the *Bismarck's* port quarter meant remaining inside the fog area; and with her early pattern radar, the *Norfolk* could not compete with mist, or other forms of low visibility. She could not rely on 'seeing' through these in the way that the *Suffolk*—and perhaps the *Bismarck*—could. Therefore when the visibility was poor, it was only too possible for her to get very close to the *Bismarck* without knowing of her proximity; a highly dangerous contingency for two reasons. If the *Bismarck* were fitted with gunnery radar, as she might well be, she would be able to open fire on and possibly sink the unseeing and unsuspecting *Norfolk* without the latter knowing the whereabouts of her assailant: though it was true the *Bismarck's* salvoes had not followed the *Norfolk* into the mist at the first sighting. But enemy radar apart, an involuntary close approach to the *Bismarck* in mist or rain would be subject to the unpleasant risk that a sudden lengthening of the visibility might leave the *Norfolk* exposed naked to view at lethal range. And if a station on the enemy's port quarter meant remaining in the mist, it would expose the *Norfolk* to precisely these hazards. However, both the Rear-Admiral and Captain Phillips were in agreement that there was nothing else to be done. Perhaps, too, the *Norfolk* would run out of the fog belt after a time. So Captain Phillips brought the *Norfolk* round, still in the mist, to what he estimated was a suitable course, based on the enemy's position and movements as reported by the *Suffolk*.

For the *Suffolk*, with her good radar, shadowing was not specially difficult, at all events to begin with, though it was exacting in that it demanded very close watchfulness. The sea was calm, and between the fog-bank and the ice the weather was clear. The distance at which to shadow required some judgment and experiment. The *Suffolk* had to be near enough to keep in touch, preferably visual touch, but far enough away to avoid coming under accurate gunfire. Even one hit might cause a reduction of her speed, which would result in the ship falling astern and losing contact with the enemy; and as the *Bismarck's* effective gun-range in good visibility, and possibly by radar in bad, was any-thing up to sixteen or seventeen miles, it was necessary to remain at a respectful distance. But since the limit of range of the *Suffolk's* radar was about thirteen miles, Captain Ellis en-deavoured to remain at about that distance.

The weather was preventing any aircraft from giving assis-tance to the surface shadowers. For several hours, however, the *Suffolk* did have an aerial escort. A large goose detached itself from a flight passing some way to the northward and flew along with the ship close over the forecastle. As the news of its pres-ence passed round the ship, several sportsmen from the ward-room, with an eye on varying the dinner menu, were for shoot-ing it down on board on the plea that it was a pro-axis goose on reconnaissance for the enemy. But Captain Ellis, with thoughts of the Ancient Mariner, restrained them.

Coastal aircraft were, however, taking off. As soon as the surface sighting reports began to come through, the Iceland Group decided to send out reconnaissance at all costs. Though it meant taking big risks, Z /201 got away from Reykjavik at 10.25 p.m., followed by L /269 at 11.18 p.m. and G /269 at 8.50 a.m.

As night approached, the surface shadowing conditions deteriorated. As seen from the *Suffolk*, the German ships began to run in and out of patches of mist. At one moment, the *Bis-marck* would be clearly in sight at thirteen or fourteen miles. A few minutes later, the weather would close in and it would be impossible to see more than a mile or two.

Then snow and rain storms began to be encountered. Such weather was obviously in the enemy's favour by giving him cover for unobserved manœuvres. It was fully to be expected that he would try to throw off pursuit by large alterations of course when good opportunities occurred. For the moment, the *Bis-marck* could only make such alterations to port, in view of the nearness of the ice on her starboard side. Later on, when more open water was reached, there would be scope for evasive tactics on both sides.

Another possibility was that the *Bismarck* might try to make an unnoticed right-about-turn to bring one or other of the shadowers within decisive gun range and so dispose of her. If this turn were made behind mist or snow, it might not be any too easy, even with radar, to spot what was happening until the range had already come down quite a lot. Without efficient radar, there would be little or no warning until the shadowing ship blundered into the returning enemy at point-blank range; as the *Norfolk* especially had to keep in mind. Indeed, but for the *Suffolk's* up-to-date equipment, Captain Ellis could hardly have held the *Bismarck* for long in the very adverse weather conditions now beginning to prevail. As it was, he had at least a fair chance of keeping a grip on her, whether she were visible or invisible from his bridge.

To add to his difficulties, mirage effects were pronounced. For instance, round about 10 p.m. the *Bismarck* was noticed to be altering course round the edge of a rainstorm, into which she shortly disappeared. A minute or two later, those on the bridge of the *Suffolk* were electrified to catch a glimpse of her apparently coming straight towards them, after which the rain again shut off the view. Of her having turned right round, everyone on the *Suffolk's* bridge was quite sure. Here was undoubtedly the very trick that had been anticipated of trying to catch the pursuers unawares. There was only one thing to do and not an instant to be lost in doing it. Over went the *Suffolk's* wheel and she swung round to the opposite course to keep her distance. Yet, as more minutes passed and the *Bismarck* did not emerge from the rain-squall as she ought to have done, it became clear that she had not turned round at all. Back the *Suffolk* went, having sacrificed four to five miles and temporarily lost touch, which it required some very hard steaming to regain.

Ten minutes before midnight, the *Bismarck* disappeared into a snowstorm. A little later, the *Suffolk* herself entered the snow and remained in it for the next three hours with visibility down to a mile. For over two hours she lost touch with the enemy,

46

but had regained radar contact by 2.50 a.m.; and at 3.20 a.m., in improving visibility, she sighted the *Bismarck* on the port bow at twelve miles. A few minutes later the light played another freak trick. The *Bismarck* was clearly seen to make a large alteration of course to starboard. Bearings were taken, but curiously enough gave a contrary result; and it soon became clear that she had, instead of a large turn to starboard, actually made a small turn to port.

Thus did the pursuit continue, chasers and chased rushing at nearly full speed through the icy waters of the Strait in the half light of the Arctic night, in and out of fog-banks, snow and rain squalls, the *Suffolk* with her radar constantly probing for the enemy and her wireless office sending out a succession of signals giving the latest estimate of the enemy's position, course and speed for the guidance of any British big ships trying to set an intercepting course.

Meanwhile, Vice-Admiral Holland's squadron of *Hood* and *Prince of Wales* with six destroyers had been steaming hard to cut the enemy off. The Vice-Admiral had taken in one of the *Suffolk's* early signals a few minutes after 8 p.m. the evening before, which had put the enemy about 300 miles nearly north (005 degrees) from the *Hood*. The Vice-Admiral calculated the intercepting course as 295 degrees and he turned his ships to that, increasing speed to 27 knots. From then till midnight, course was adjusted in the light of the *Suffolk's* enemy reports. At midnight, the *Bismarck* was estimated to be 120 miles away, bearing 010 degrees, and the Vice-Admiral expected to make contact any time after 1.40 a.m.[1] At fifteen minutes past midnight, therefore, he ordered all ships to make final preparations for action and to hoist battle ensigns. Officers and men went clambering into their action stations and for a quarter of an hour the telephone systems of the big ships were alive with voices passing orders and making reports, as all the turret and gun machinery and other battle equipment was tested and got ready for instant use.

---

[1] It is difficult to understand how he can have expected so early a contact, as the rate of relative approach was under 35 knots.

All-Night Shadowing and a Dawn Battle

At this time, however, the flow of enemy reports ceased to come in, due to the *Bismarck* and *Suffolk* running into the snow-storm, and half an hour after midnight the Vice-Admiral signalled to the *Prince of Wales* that if the enemy was not seen by ten minutes past two, he would probably steer parallel to him till the cruisers regained touch, so as to make sure the enemy did not get ahead of the British squadron unsighted. Accordingly, at the time mentioned, the Vice-Admiral turned back to about south-south-west and reduced speed. Men not on watch were told that they could sleep at their action stations; but so tense was the feeling of expectancy that few of them did. For some reason, the Vice-Admiral told his destroyers to continue to the north-ward when the big ships turned south-south-west.

On receiving the *Suffolk's* report of regaining touch at 2.47 the Vice-Admiral brought his ships round again for a closing course and went on to 28 knots. Visibility was poor. There was a fresh breeze from the starboard side and a moderate swell. By 4 a.m., the enemy was estimated to be twenty miles to the north-west. Visibility was beginning to improve as twilight lightened into day. By 4.30 a.m. it was twelve miles and increasing. At 5.10 a.m. instant readiness for action was ordered; and at 5.35 a.m. two ships were made out a long way off before the starboard beam. The heavy turrets, which were waiting silent but alert, sprang into movement as they followed the Director round in that direction.

It was the German squadron. The enemy ships were some way apart, so that the two vessels could not be held in the spotting officers' glasses simultaneously.[1] The silhouettes of both looked very similar, and in the *Prince of Wales's* after control tower it was thought at first that they were the *Bismarck* and *Tirpitz*. Vice-Admiral Holland had made an excellent contact, his force being nicely on the enemy's bow. Two minutes after the sighting, he turned both his ships 40 degrees towards the enemy to shorten the range. The turn was made by Blue Pendant (i.e. both ships turning together as the signal came down), and it closed the British A arcs; that is to say, the bearing of the enemy was now

[1] Noted by Sub-Lieut. G. A. G. Brooke in the *Prince of Wales's* after control.

4. Admiral Tovey and Staff pacing the flagship's deck. (*Right*) The Admiral; (*Centre*) Flag-Captain W. R. Patterson; (*Left*) Commodore E. J. P. Brind, Chief of Staff

5. H.M.S. *Hood* in harbour at Scapa shortly before the operation

6. H.M.S. *Suffolk* on patrol in the Denmark Strait

7. The pack ice in the Denmark Strait as seen from H.M.S. *Norfolk*

too far ahead for the after turrets to bear: to the disgust of their crews and those in the after controls, to whom it was desperately tantalizing to have their view of the enemy shut off at this supreme moment. Twelve minutes later, the ships were turned another 20 degrees towards the enemy.

In the *Norfolk* and *Suffolk*, too, excitement was mounting. The cruisers had not become aware until 4.45 a.m., from an intercepted signal by one of Vice-Admiral Holland's destroyers, that British heavy ships were in the vicinity. At a quarter past five, the *Norfolk* sighted two smudges of smoke on the port bow, which gradually took shape as the *Hood* and *Prince of Wales* steaming at high speed towards the enemy, who had also now come in sight sixteen miles on the starboard bow. The *Suffolk* had also seen the British battle force, and for those on both cruisers' bridges its appearance made a most gladsome sight. They had had a tense and anxious night, racing along behind the enemy under most difficult weather conditions, while their signals guided their bigger brothers to the scene. Now the big ships had actually arrived, the cruisers' object had been successfully achieved, and their tired officers and men prepared to watch with joyful and fascinated satisfaction the outcome of their efforts in the shape of the destruction of the enemy. Little did they realize what they were about to see.

From now onwards, things happened very quickly. At 5.49 a.m., the Vice-Admiral made the signal for a concentration on the left-hand ship. He had clearly mistaken the *Prinz Eugen* for the *Bismarck*, as they realized at once in the *Prince of Wales* where, the Captain and the Gunnery Officer being both certain the *Bismarck* was the right-hand ship, it was decided to disregard the signal. Three minutes later, when the range was down to 25,000 yards, the Vice-Admiral evidently discovered the mistake and made the signal for shifting one target right, Almost at the same moment, the *Hood* opened fire, to which the *Bismarck* at once replied. Within a matter of seconds, the *Prince of Wales* had joined in and the action had begun. Which ship was the *Bismarck* firing at? After a rather tense wait for the time of flight to pass, those in the *Prince of Wales* noted, not without relief, that she was firing at the *Hood*.[1]

The principal guide posts in modern naval gun battles, both for the actual combatants and for any observers, are the splashes made by shells hitting the water. These splashes leap up to a great height—in the case of large shells to about 200 feet—and are the means whereby gun control officers know where their shots are going. If all the splashes are over or short or to the right or to the left of the target the appropriate corrections are applied. What the control officer wants is a 'straddle'; that is to say, one or more splashes over and one or more splashes short. He then knows that he is 'on' the target and that there may be one or more hits. As a rule, he will not—indeed he should not— see those hits. With delay-action fuses, a shell may crash through a ship's side or deck and penetrate deep into her hull before exploding. When, therefore, it does go off, the flash will probably be right inside the ship and invisible from outside. At Jutland, in 1916, those British officers and men who were in the open were cheered by the sight of big golden explosions on the ships of the High Seas Fleet. Had they known, the fact that they could see those explosions meant that the British shells were going off at the first touch and without penetration.

As seen from the distant *Norfolk* and *Suffolk*, the *Hood's* firing seemed excellent. Her first two salvoes were very close to the enemy and the third looked like a straddle. The *Prince of Wales* was taking longer to get on. Her first salvo was over. Corrections were made, but it was not until the sixth salvo that a straddle was obtained. As already mentioned, the ship had gone into action with only her forward turrets (A and B) bearing on the enemy, owing to the ship's acute angle of inclination to the line of fire on the closing course being steered. One of A turret's guns, moreover, had a temporary defect which made it certain that, although it could fire the one round with which it was loaded, it would fire no more until the ship got back to harbour. This was known beforehand to both the Gunnery Officer and the Captain. Range-finding during the approach had been difficult. A and B turret rangefinders were blanked by spray, and

[1] For a plan of the action see Diagram 2.

fire had had to be opened on the strength of the comparatively small (15-ft.) rangefinder in the Director Control Tower. Hence the initial overestimating of the range by about 1,000 yards.

The cruisers themselves were out of range. The *Suffolk* did try half a dozen salvoes, but they all fell a long way short. Her gun-flashes showed up her position to the *Norfolk*, away on the enemy's other quarter; which was the first time the *Suffolk* had been in sight from the cruiser flagship since they had parted company at Isafiord, the morning before.

The *Bismarck* and *Prinz Eugen* both opened against the *Hood* and were both quickly on to their target. With her more rapid rate of fire, the *Prinz Eugen* scored the first hit in under a minute. A large fire broke out by the *Hood's* mainmast which spread rapidly forward and blazed up high above the upper deck. To the watchers in the cruisers, it appeared as a big semicircle of flame, very like the top half of a setting sun, and they held their breath wondering whether it would be humanly possible to get it under control. Then it died down somewhat and afterwards seemed to pulsate up and down.

The *Bismarck* was showing no similar signs of damage. But after about three minutes of battle, the *Norfolk's* people saw something which convinced them that she had just been hit by a heavy shell. Having up till then been making no smoke to speak of, she suddenly emitted a conspicuous pillar of black smoke out of her funnel. It was as if, shaken by some heavy jolt, all the soot had fallen out of the crevices and corners of her boiler-room uptakes and been shot high into the air on the escaping funnel gases.

In the *Prince of Wales* the Spotting Officer, Lieutenant-Commander A. G. Skipwith, was puzzled at not noticing any splashes from the *Hood* going up near the *Bismarck*. Throughout the action he never removed his eyes from his high-powered gunnery binoculars which were continuously and automatically trained on the *Bismarck*, but saw no splashes but those of his own ship. He had expected to be confused by the *Hood's* splashes and was therefore all the more struck at seeing none. Possibly, the firing of the *Prince of Wales's* own salvoes, accompanied as it would be by the emission of great clouds of brown cordite smoke, happened to coincide with the fall of the *Hood's* shells, thus momentarily obscuring the control officers' view of the *Hood's* splashes. Such exact synchronization, however, though quite conceivable for an odd salvo or two, would be very unlikely for every one. Moreover, the head wind was blowing the cordite smoke clear almost at once and gave plenty of time to see large shell splashes, which would remain visible for an appreciable time, fired by another ship. Was it possible that the *Hood* was not firing at the *Bismarck*.[1]

The range meanwhile was coming down rapidly. At 5.55 a.m. the Vice-Admiral made the signal for a Blue Pendant turn of 20 degrees to port, away from the enemy. This would have opened both ships' A arcs and have brought the squadron's full gunpower to bear. By now, the *Bismarck* had obtained several straddles on the *Hood*, and had very probably hit her. The German Admiral, perhaps fearing to leave one enemy ship wholly unfired-at and also possibly to eliminate splash interference in spotting the fall of shot, had just ordered the *Prinz Eugen* to switch her fire to the other target.

As the British ships began their turn, two German splashes went up close alongside the *Hood*. Almost immediately, the horrified spectators in the British cruisers saw a vast eruption of flame leap upwards between the *Hood's* masts to a height of many hundreds of feet, perhaps as high as a thousand, in the middle of which a great incandescent ball was seen soaring skywards. The volcanic upshoot of fire lasted but a second or two; and when it had disappeared the place where the *Hood* had been was covered by an enormous column of smoke. Through it, the bows and stern of the ship could just be discerned, each rising steeply up as the central part of the ship collapsed. The *Hood* had blown up in the middle, had broken in half, and in a couple of minutes or so had completely disappeared. The *Prince of Wales*, who was already swinging in obedience to the turning signal, had to reverse her rudder quickly and sheer back to starboard to avoid the pillar of smoke and the probable wreckage within it.

---

[1] This question is discussed further in a later part of this chapter.

52

May 24th

The *Prince of Wales* had been firing away at the *Bismarck* almost undisturbed during the few minutes in which the *Hood* had been drawing the enemy's fire. She now came in for the full blast of the enemy's ferocity. A towering wall of water leapt out of the sea close at hand, where a 15-in. salvo had landed. It was swiftly followed by the slightly smaller splashes of the *Bismarck's* secondary armament 6-in. shells, salvoes of which, mingling with and scarcely distinguishable from those of the *Prinz Eugen's* 8-in., began to fall one on top of the other with whirlwind rapidity about every ten to fifteen seconds. The din was tremendous, the rush and crash of the enemy's shells combining with the roar and banging of the *Prince of Wales's* heavy and light guns and the hiss of falling spray from nearby shell splashes to make what seemed a continuous deluge of sound. So much water was being thrown up all around *Prince of Wales*, some of it reaching up over the masthead, that it became none too easy to spot her own fall of shot. Every now and then the ship was felt to shudder as something hit her, and those in the after control became aware of black smoke drifting past them from an obvious fire further forward. In the midst of this turmoil, a 15-in. shell came streaking down on to the bridge, through which it smashed, exploding just as it emerged on the other side. The bridge instantly became a shambles, every officer and man on that key position being either killed or wounded, excepting only Captain Leach himself and the Chief Yeoman of Signals, though both were knocked down and momentarily dazed. In the plotting-room just below, blood began to drip off the end of the bridge voicepipe on to the plot. Curiously enough, the Gunnery Officer and other main control officers in the Director Tower, a few feet only from this explosion, entirely failed to notice it and continued to direct the ship's fire with undivided concentration of purpose.[1]

[1] The ship received seven hits during this period—four 15-in. and three 8-in. The shell on the bridge, as well as the damage it did there, severed the communications to the steering wheel and destroyed some of the gunnery control telephone leads. Another 15-in. hit the superstructure supporting the Fore Secondary Armament (5·5-in.) Directors and put them out of action, and the after Director took over. The third hit went off on the aircraft crane. The ship's aircraft was on the point of being catapulted off to act as gunnery spotter. The catapult

All-Night Shadowing and a Dawn Battle

To make matters worse, the *Prince of Wales's* newness was now telling against her. Small mechanical breakdowns kept occurring in the turrets, now one gun and now another missing a salvo or two. The building firm's foremen of the turrets, who had been living on board completing their assemblage and the final adjustment of the equipment, had come to sea with the ship and were in the turrets at this time. These men, with their intimate knowledge of the machinery, were doing invaluable work in helping to rectify the mishaps that were taking place. But even so the average salvo was of about three guns, instead of five. To Captain Leach, who by now had moved to the lower bridge, the fact that his ship was not developing her full gun-power was obvious. He knew that mechanical troubles might be expected with the new type of mounting fitted in his ship; one gun, as he was aware, being completely out of action. He knew that his ship's company were semi-trained. His vessel was under a heavy and accurate fire from an enemy which had just blown up his flagship before his eyes. That enemy, on the other hand, showed no apparent sign of damage but was still shooting very accurately with, as it seemed, all her guns in action. Captain Leach had to consider whether the combination of adverse factors gave him adequate prospects of continuing the action with sufficient hope of success. He was aware that there was every likelihood of tactical reinforcement before long, and it is therefore understandable that he came to the swift conclusion that he ought to wait for it and that the present engagement should be broken off. With the range down to not much more than 14,000 yards, he put his wheel over and retired out of action behind a

officer actually had his flag in the air preparatory to dropping it for the signal to go when the shell arrived. When he had picked himself up, he saw that both wings of the aircraft had been shattered by splinters; so getting the crew out, he hastily catapulted the dangerous, petrol-laden wreck into the sea. Not till the ship returned to harbour was it discovered that yet another heavy shell had pierced the side deep under water, had passed through several protecting bulkheads, and had come to rest without exploding close to one of the diesel dynamo rooms. Two of the 8-in. hits had been on the waterline aft. The ship's side was pierced and a number of compartments were flooded, about 500 tons of water getting into the ship. The third 8-in. shell entered one of the 5·25-in. shell handing-rooms. Round this small space it flew like lightning several times and eventually sat down without going off and without having touched a man.

smoke screen. As the *Prince of Wales* heeled over on the turn, Y turret shell ring slid over on its rollers and jammed. This left the four guns of this turret with only two more rounds apiece until the jam could be cleared.

The turn-away obscured the view of the main gun control position. The after control, which should have taken over, could not do so because the layer's view was fogged by the smoke screen, and the control officers' glasses, which had been drenched by the falling spray of a shell splash, were being feverishly wiped dry. The officer of Y turret, finding no orders coming through, decided he ought to take over in local control and got off his last eight rounds on his own. But his estimate of the range and other essential data could only be rough, and according to the *Norfolk* and *Suffolk* the salvoes fell a long way from the enemy.[1]

The *Bismarck* made no attempt to follow the *Prince of Wales*, but was seen to alter course away as the *Prince of Wales* turned.

It remains to examine the question of which British ships were firing at which German. It seems to be beyond dispute that the *Prince of Wales* was shooting at the *Bismarck*. But what of the *Hood*?

It has already been mentioned that the *Prince of Wales's* spotting officer saw no splashes near the *Bismarck* but those of his own ship. There can also be no doubt that the Vice-Admiral and others in the *Hood* initially mistook the *Prinz Eugen* for the *Bismarck*; and that this error was only realized, as we know from the concentration signal, a second or two before opening fire. It is possible that this last minute change of target did not reach the *Hood's* gun control tower before fire was opened. It is also possible that, even if it did, the very close similarity of the two German ships' silhouettes and the fact that only one German ship was visible at a time in the gunnery spotting and laying glasses may have deceived the *Hood's* Director Layer into thinking he was on the right-hand ship when he was actually on the left-hand one.

[1] From first to last, the *Prince of Wales* fired eighteen main armament salvoes.

All-Night Shadowing and a Dawn Battle

On the other hand, those on board the *Norfolk* and the *Suffolk*, twelve to fifteen miles away on the quarters of the *Bismarck*, were quite sure the *Hood* was firing at the *Bismarck* and was making accurate shooting. But, in fact, while the cruisers' positions a long way nearly astern of the *Bismarck* made it easy for their people to judge how the British salvoes were falling for range, it was equally difficult for them to estimate from that angle how they were falling for 'line'; that is, to the right or the left of the target from the point of view of the firing ship. As seen from the two British cruisers, the *Bismarck* and *Prinz Eugen* were almost in line with each other, and it was therefore hardly possible to be certain at which German ship the British salvoes were being aimed.

There is a certain amount of evidence from the German side bearing on the subject. A German official account of the action, written in 1942, and subsequently found among captured war documents, indicates that both the *Bismarck* and *Prinz Eugen* were under fire. The relevant extract is as follows:

'*Prinze Eugen* was lucky in the fight, as she received no hits, although shots from the *heavy artillery* were observed on all sides in the immediate vicinity of the ship. Contrary to the tactical rules in force, neither the Commander-in-Chief of the fleet nor the Captain of the ship which, according to her armour strength, should be classed as a light craft, had ordered her to withdraw to the lee of the fire at the beginning of the battle. She had, therefore, remained in the line.

'This deviation from our tactical rules was apparently caused by the fact that the British ships, approaching head-on, were first reported as heavy cruisers; and this deviation was adhered to later when the enemy was recognized as a formation of battleships. The latter was thereby forced to *spread his fire*.'

If the *Prinz Eugen* was, in fact, under fire as well as the *Bismarck* from heavy artillery, then clearly the two British ships must have been firing at different targets, since the *Bismarck* and *Prinz Eugen* would seem to have been too far apart for stray shots aimed at one to fall near the other. For that case, the evidence of the original error in the Vice-Admiral's concentration signal suggests that if one or other of the British big ships was firing at the *Prinz Eugen* it was more probably the *Hood* than the *Prince of Wales*. But in his signal to the German shore authorities, Admiral Lutjens of the *Bismarck* (Fuehrer naval conferences 1941, p. 76) said that: '*Hood* concentrated fire on the *Bismarck*,' but also that '*Bismarck* received two hits from *King George*.'[1] Since these are the only hits mentioned by him, it follows that in the German Admiral's opinion the *Hood* did not hit the *Bismarck* at all.

How could he have known? One possibility is that the *Bismarck* was not hit till after the *Hood* had blown up. Also the Germans had a system of 'battle observers' with stop watches whose duty it was to observe the enemy's fire and identify the different salvoes. The German Admiral could have known which British ship was hitting the *Bismarck* either by this means or because the *Hood* was firing at the *Prinz Eugen* or through the *Bismarck* not being hit before the *Hood* had gone. Which of these alternatives is the right one is a matter for conjecture. What is indisputable is that the *Bismarck* herself said that the hits on her came from the *Prince of Wales*.

AUTHOR'S NOTE

Since the above was written, the author has received information from German sources that the *Hood* was, in fact, firing at the *Prinz Eugen*.

---

[1] Which means *Prince of Wales*.

CHAPTER 4

The Admiralty Takes some Vigorous Steps

The blowing up of the *Hood* came as a shock to the whole Navy. She was the biggest ship in the fleet. During the majority of the inter-war years, she had been generally reckoned, in respect of the combination of fighting power, speed and protection, to be the most powerful ship in the world. Practically a whole generation of naval men had grown up to regard her with something like awe as the very embodiment of naval strength. In fleet manœuvres over many years, when the 'mighty *Hood*' appeared on the scene, the other side's chances were felt to be as good as over. And in her first battle she had disintegrated in a huge burst of flame after being under fire for only a few minutes.

Moreover, her fate was unpleasantly reminiscent of what had happened at Jutland when four British armoured ships had also gone up in flames that leapt skywards as the magazines exploded. It was afterwards said that better protection in future ships and the fitting of anti-flash devices in the magazines would prevent further disasters of this kind. Now it had happened again.

As might be expected, excuses for the calamitous occurrence began to appear in public print. Some commentators merely put it down to a lucky hit. Others ascribed it to the *Hood* being more than twenty years old, or alternatively to her being a 'battle cruiser'. It was, of course, quite true that both naval science and naval weapons had developed considerably since the *Hood* was first commissioned. Yet naval officers had an uncomfortable feeling that the *Hood* disaster could not legitimately be explained away on those grounds. For it was not a new weapon such as the airborne 'blockbuster' that had destroyed the ship but the old-established gun projectile which had been the standard weapon at the time the *Hood* was designed and for long before. Moreover, although some aspects of warship design, such as the engineering side, had undoubtedly made notable strides since the *Hood's* launch, gunnery and shell manufacture were not very different in 1941 from what they had been in 1918. If, then, the *Hood*, with 15-in. guns herself, blew up in action with another 15-in. gun ship on the later date, she might well have done so on the earlier. In other words, she had been too weak to fight from the beginning: for the least that can be asked of a warship is that she should be able to stand up to an enemy of similar offensive strength.

Nor was it accurate to ascribe the *Hood's* weakness to her being a 'battle cruiser'. For any given tonnage, a ship can support a certain total weight of combined armament, armour protection and propulsive machinery, and no more. The bigger the share, therefore, that is allotted to any one of these battle components of guns, armour and speed, the less there is available for the other two. The pre-Jutland battle cruisers were of approximately the same tonnage as contemporary battleships, and as their speed was considerably higher their armament and armour had to be correspondingly lower. These ships were thoroughly under-protected as the Jutland battle lamentably showed. The *Hood*, the first post-Jutland big ship, had the same main armament (eight 15-in. guns) as the latest class of battleship at the time of her launch, and had a much higher speed. Had she therefore been of the same tonnage, her protection must necessarily have been inferior to theirs. But she was not of the same tonnage. On the contrary, whereas the *Revenge* displaced 29,000 tons odd, she displaced no less than 42,000; and her extra size made possible a comparable degree of protection. At the time she was built, there was no limitation on battleship size, and the *Hood* could, if necessary, have been made even larger in order to make her battleworthy.

The Admiralty Takes Some Vigorous Steps

The undoubted fact is that her design was defective. Indeed, a year or two after her launch certain naval experts drew attention to the circumstance that an enemy shell approaching a certain part of the ship at a certain angle would have a fairly easy passage into a magazine. This weakness could, however, be remedied by extra armour plating, and the higher authorities at the Admiralty decided to have this placed when the next opportunity came for an extensive refit. But time passed and the job was not done. There were other ships needing reconstruction just as much as the *Hood*. Money was short and even though the 'twenties and early 'thirties were years of allegedly profound peace, too many ships could not be laid up at once. Then came the Abyssinian crisis, and after that it became difficult to take the *Hood* in hand for extensive alteration for the opposite reason. She was such a big and well-known ship to put out of commission during the years of growing international tension, and political influence was on the side of her remaining in normal service. So the job was never done.

The action had been fought on the British side with inelastic formalism. The two ships had come into action in close order and had been manœuvred as one by signal from the flagship. It was an arrangement which left next to no initiative in the hands of the Captain of the *Prince of Wales*. He was an able and experienced officer, specially trained since boyhood to fight a warship in action, for which he was fully qualified by rank, seniority and technical knowledge. Yet, when the time came, he was given no scope. He was told what courses to steer, what ship to fire at, what speed to maintain, and when to open fire.

The advantage of this shackling of talent is not apparent from an analysis of the tactics employed. There were two British capital ships against one German. The *Hood* had an equal number of heavy guns to the *Bismarck* and of the same calibre. The *Prince of Wales* had two more guns of slightly smaller calibre, though one of them would go out of action after the first round. Taken together, but leaving this gun out, the British ships had seventeen heavy guns to the German eight, a superiority of at least two to one.

60

The Admiralty Takes Some Vigorous Steps

Owing, however, to the way the British ships came into action, this superiority was not brought into play. When the action opened, the *Bismarck* had her full broadside of eight guns bearing. But Vice-Admiral Holland was intent on closing the range quickly, and was steering inwards at a steep angle with the *Hood's* A arcs closed; that is, with only her two foremost turrets able to fire. The *Prince of Wales*, obliged by signal to conform to the *Hood's* movements, was similarly placed with only six of her ten guns bearing, one of which would only fire one round. This was the position during nearly the whole period the two British ships were together, until the *Hood* blew up. Thus, during this first critical part of the action only nine British guns were facing eight German, so that the British superiority was almost entirely thrown away. The remaining eight British guns were held in reserve so long that their influence was never exerted; for almost before the signal which would have swung them into action could take effect, one of the British ships had ceased to fight.[1]

With the *Hood's* destruction, the *Prince of Wales's* close proximity to her also became a drawback. It was then easy for the *Bismarck* to switch her guns through the one or two degrees of bearing that had separated the *Prince of Wales* from the *Hood*, while the gun range that had finished off the latter would be approximately right for the *Prince of Wales*, too. Had the *Prince of Wales* been, say, a couple of miles from the *Hood* and at a range of her own Captain's choosing, the German transfer of target would have been lengthier and less simple. Moreover, if Captain Leach had enjoyed independent freedom of manœuvre, the closing of both ships' A arcs at the same time could have been avoided. If a quick closing of the range had then still been desired, it could have been done by each ship alternately moving in and sacrificing her full gunfire, while the other kept her broadside open to cover her consort's advance.

Close proximity also enhanced the moral effect of the *Hood's* explosion. Lieutenant-Commander McMullen, the ship's gun-

---

[1] If the *Hood* was, in fact, firing at the *Prinz Eugen*, only five British 14-in. guns will have been opposed to eight German 15-in.

nery officer, suddenly noticed that the inside walls of the Gunnery Director Tower, his battle station, were tinted a lurid orange, and guessed from this and the roar of the explosion what was happening. No doubt originating in the same way, the news went round the ship in a flash. In a matter of seconds, McMullen heard in his control telephone the voice of the 'dagger' Gunner[1] in the transmitting station, 100 feet down inside the ship, saying to him: 'How's the *Hood*, sir?' 'She's not too good.' 'She's gone hasn't she, sir?'

On the face of it, the British tactics appear to have been unskilfully conceived and directed. Yet Vice-Admiral Holland was regarded in high esteem throughout the Navy as an officer of outstanding ability. He had, moreover, done well in the Mediterranean in the earlier period of the war. What, then, is likely to have induced him to pursue the course of action that he did?

Was he following Sir John Tovey's principle of the end-on approach which the latter invariably propounded to every flag and commanding officer who joined his fleet? This was a speciality of the Commander-in-Chief's, and was based on the idea that if A arcs had to be sacrificed in order to close the range quickly, the safest way to do it was to steer absolutely straight for the enemy without regard to loss of bearing. An end-on approach shortened the danger period when A arcs were closed and also reduced the lateral target presented by the approaching ship to the width of her beam—say 100 feet. This compared with a target of, for a big ship, about 600 to 700 feet when broadside on. Of course, when the lateral target was thus reduced, the longitudinal target, along the line of fire, was automatically increased. But it was Sir John Tovey's belief that the lateral target mattered a lot more than the longitudinal, observation of numerous practice firings having convinced him that there was more likelihood of missing a target for 'line' (to the right or the left) than for range (over or short). Hence, on balance, a ship end-on would be more difficult to hit than a ship broadside

---

[1] Some Naval Gunners (Warrant Officers) who undergo an advanced gunnery course, have a distinctive † put against their names in the Navy List. They are invariably known as dagger Gunners.

on. But an essential condition of reaping this advantage was that the approach should be completely end-on.[1] With any deviation to the right or left, the advantage falls disproportionately away. A deviation, for instance, of 30 degrees (a third of a right angle) does not increase a ship's lateral target by a third but by a half.

Now, Vice-Admiral Holland was not pointing end-on to the *Bismarck*. He was steering about 30 degrees away from that line. From the point of view of the 'Tovey' approach theory, therefore, he had the worst of both worlds. His A arcs were closed and only half his gunpower was being employed: but at the same time he was presenting a comparatively broad target to the enemy's fire. It must, therefore, be considered doubtful whether he had the Commander-in-Chief's end-on theory in mind at all. Examining the evidence later on in harbour, Sir John Tovey came to the conclusion that he had not.[2]

The other possibility is that the Vice-Admiral was basing his tactics on the printed fighting instructions; and here the facts are in much closer correspondence with supposition. The author has been assured by senior officers that the way the Vice-Admiral took his squadron into action harmonized with some fidelity with the official instructions as to how such a phase of a battle should be conducted. It is therefore possible that he was, in fact, following on those instructions.

The instructions to which reference is here made were the descendants of the old Fighting Instructions of the seventeenth and eighteenth centuries, and had many features in common with these their forebears, notably in their centralizing character. The generality of Admirals of the earlier centuries liked to keep the control of the battle in their own hands as far as they could, and the official Fighting Instructions issued for the guidance of subordinate Commanders always tended towards a tactical rigidity and formality of manœuvre with little initiative left to

---

[1] Sir John Tovey regarded anything within 10° either side of right ahead permissible.

[2] When Sir John Tovey was discussing the action with the First Sea Lord, the latter expressed criticism of the steep angle at which the Vice-Admiral had steered in towards the enemy. Sir John replied that he wished he had been steering in more still.

juniors. Nelson's rare genius virtually killed these cut-and-dried fighting rules for a century. The brilliant unorthodoxy of his methods and his open contempt for tactical convention, as well as his persistent encouragement of all his juniors to exercise their own independent initiative were obviously inconsistent with voluminous printed instructions; and the British Navy, nurtured during the nineteenth century on the simple Nelsonian precept that 'no Captain can do very wrong who places his ship alongside that of an enemy', went into the war of 1914 with practically none.

There was an immediate reversion to ancient practice. A new set of battle instructions was compiled, just as bulky as any of its predecessors and breathing a very similar spirit of centralized control. These new Instructions, with minor alterations, remained the tactical 'Bible' of the Navy from 1918 till the outbreak of war in 1939, and were officially taught to numerous courses of senior officers at the Tactical School. There could, therefore, be no great cause for surprise if Vice-Admiral Holland's actions were governed by these instructions on 24th May 1941; and if a noteworthy lack of success attended his tactics that day, any criticisms arising therefrom must attach not to him but to the official Instructions which probably inspired his conduct. Though a man can deservedly earn praise for successfully defying his instructions, he cannot legitimately be blamed for obeying them. The point of principal remark is that such defective official instructions should have retained the approval of successive Boards of Admiralty for a generation.

Why was it necessary for the range to be shortened so quickly that A arcs had to be closed? It would surely seem that if the *Bismarck* was capable of decisive gunfire at 25,000 yards, the British big ships should have been equally able to fight at that range. Indeed, they almost certainly were. The *Bismarck* was well within their gun range, and since they were firing at her with half their guns they could obviously have fired at her with all. The use of their full broadsides was not incompatible with a closing range: the only condition was that closing with A arcs open meant closing a little more slowly. But it was early morn-

64

ing and the British ships had plenty of time. Why then the hurry to get in? The answer is not very obvious.

It remains to be said that the *Bismarck's* shooting was brilliant. Her fire control was extremely good and her spread of salvoes very small indeed; her standard in this respect being far higher than the British Navy could then show.[1] Her achievement on this occasion was remarkable. Faced by a two-to-one enemy superiority, in five or six salvoes she had blown up one ship and in another twelve or so had driven the other out of action.

The defeat of the *Hood's* detachment threw numerous plans into the melting-pot. But on two men in particular, Admiral Tovey and Rear-Admiral Wake-Walker, it imposed the need for a drastic and urgent re-shaping of their ideas. Half an hour before, the latter had been the leader of shadowing forces which, after trailing a powerful enemy all night, had just handed that enemy over to a superior officer for destruction. Rear-Admiral Wake-Walker must have felt a pleasant glow of satisfaction at having thus brought a very tricky task to a successful conclusion; and, with his own responsibility lessened by the arrival of an Admiral senior to himself, have prepared to take a spectator's enjoyment in the last thrilling act of a drama, in the initial stages of which he had played a leading part.

The brilliant flash of a huge explosion had changed the situation in an instant. As the flame and smoke from the shattered *Hood* towered upwards, the Rear-Admiral realized that he was once again the senior officer on the spot and that the burden of his previous responsibility had fallen back upon his shoulders. Once more he was in sole charge of the forces in immediate contact with the enemy. Moreover, the state of affairs was now substantially different from what it had previously been or indeed from anything he had anticipated. Before, he had been guiding what he assumed to be a superior force into contact with the escaping enemy. The supposedly superior force had made contact but had proved to be inferior. The whole situation

---

[1] The Germans had manifested the same gunnery superiority in the previous war. What one Navy can do, another can. But for some reason the British gunnery had remained behind the German during the inter-war period.

had to be appreciated afresh: and it took a little time to do it.

First of all, his strength had been augmented by the important addition of one battleship and six destroyers. The latter, however, were twenty to thirty miles astern and the best thing he could do with them was to send them to look for survivors from the *Hood*. They searched a wide area for a long time, but though they encountered much wreckage, they could only find three survivors alive in the water. These were Midshipman W. J. Dundas, who had been midshipman of the watch on the upper bridge; Able Seaman R. E. Tilburn, who had been on the boat deck; and Ordinary Signalman A. E. Briggs, who had been on duty on the navigating bridge. On completion of this mournful duty, the destroyers returned to Iceland.

Out of the *Hood's* squadron, Rear-Admiral Wake-Walker had therefore only the *Prince of Wales* remaining with him. But, even so, with her and his two cruisers he was now superior in force to the enemy: on paper at least. A great deal hinged, however, on the condition of the *Prince of Wales*. The Rear-Admiral had just seen her haul out of action, pouring out masses of black smoke, and heeling so far over under helm that she looked almost as if she were capsizing. He had likewise noted that her gunfire had been somewhat ragged, her salvoes mostly consisting of three instead of five guns, while her last shots had looked very wild.[1] He guessed that, being a brand-new ship, she was having mechanical breakdowns, in which case they might well happen again were the action to be renewed; and a ship whose guns cannot fire through internal defects is just as helpless as one which has been battered into silence by the enemy. He was not, therefore, surprised when she signalled that a number of her turret guns were temporarily out of action. In addition, she reported her bridge severely damaged, 400 tons of water in the ship and her speed reduced to about 27 knots. She had been closing the *Norfolk* since hauling out of action; and the Rear-Admiral signalled to her to follow him at her best speed.

Had the *Bismarck* herself suffered damage sufficient to compensate for the *Prince of Wales's* weaknesses? Rear-Admiral

[1] He did not, of course, know that Y turret was then firing in local control.

Wake-Walker had as yet no reason to think so. He had watched her firing with great accuracy and effect during the whole of the action with the *Hood* and the *Prince of Wales*. It was obvious, therefore, that the *Bismarck's* offensive power remained of a high order. Whether her efficiency had been reduced in any other respects he could not tell. He had observed British salvoes straddling her, but he himself would not like to be certain she had been hit, though one or two of his officers had thought they had seen hits upon her. There had, it is true, been that huge burst of black smoke from her funnel. No doubt that was the result of a heavy jolt of some sort, and was quite possibly caused by a large shell burst on board. But what that shell had done in the way of damage was another matter. Experience of the previous war warned him against optimism that was not supported by irrefutable evidence.

The situation therefore seemed to be that, even with the addition of the *Prince of Wales*, his force was probably inferior to the German squadron. Were he able to compel an action, there was no certainty that he would be able to inflict serious, let alone mortal damage, on the *Bismarck*; while, on the other hand, there was the obvious risk that the British shadowing ships might be so damaged as to lose touch, if indeed the *Bismarck* did not send one or more of them to follow the *Hood*. Moreover, there was no guarantee that the British squadron could force an action at all, with the *Prince of Wales's* speed down to 27 knots. The *Bismarck* had continued to steam at high speed for some time after breaking off the action, and although the *Suffolk* reported just before eight o'clock that the enemy had reduced speed and was on fire, no sign of this fire could be seen from *Norfolk*, who made the enemy's speed still about 28 knots. A Sunderland flying boat which had made its appearance some time previously, reported, when asked, that she could see no fire and even said that the enemy was steaming at 30 knots, though this was an evident over-estimate.[1] Even, moreover, if the

---

[1] This was Z/201, the first aircraft to take off the night before. Of the other two, L/269 made no sighting and G/269, though she saw the battle, was unable through poor visibility and low clouds to identify any of the ships.

enemy had reduced speed, this reduction was not necessarily connected with action damage but might well have come from considerations of fuel economy. The enemy's original high speed had presumably been for the purpose of avoiding interception. Interception had now taken place and the intercepting force beaten off with loss. The *Bismarck* might therefore be thinking that, having dealt satisfactorily with one such force, there was no other to be reckoned with, at all events for the time being, and that she could now afford to take things more easily.

The *Suffolk* had, as a matter of fact, reported an hour and a half after the action that the *Bismarck* had reduced to 22 knots and was leaving a broad track of oil behind her. This report was not, however, received in the *Norfolk*. The same oil track was seen and reported by the Sunderland flying boat, Z/201. Unfortunately, she used the ambiguous phrase 'Losing oil', and as she herself had been under anti-aircraft fire from the *Bismarck* and shortly after making her signal had broken off her patrol and disappeared, it was assumed on board the *Norfolk* that it was her own oil that was being lost and that this was the reason for her departure. It was not till the afternoon that the Rear-Admiral learnt about the *Bismarck's* oily wake, and only then by reason of a signal thoughtfully broadcast to the British forces by the Naval-Officer-in-Charge, Iceland, based on the verbal report of the crew of the Sunderland flying boat after it had returned to its base.

Weighing up all the evidence in his possession immediately after the action, the Rear-Admiral eventually came to the conclusion that his best plan was not to work for a decisive action, which he would in any case be rather unlikely to bring to a successful issue, but to continue shadowing the enemy with a view to bringing about a further meeting between the latter and other British heavy units: and that this conclusion was the right one can hardly be doubted. The Rear-Admiral was in a better position to shadow than before, since now that he had the *Prince of Wales* with him, the *Bismarck* could no longer endeavour to drive off or cripple the shadowing cruisers without herself coming under heavy shellfire. After the *Hood's* destruction, the Rear-

Admiral had reported it to the Commander-in-Chief and Admiralty. His signal was a brief and laconic message of four words: '*Hood* has blown up', followed by the geographical position. As the Flag-Captain heard it being dictated, he found himself trying to picture the reactions that the receipt of this shattering news would cause at the Admiralty and in the *King George V.*

Whatever Sir John Tovey may have thought in his innermost mind at the news of this major set-back, which threw his whole plan out of gear, his only expressions of regret were confined to sorrow at the loss of the *Hood's* ship's company. Otherwise, his whole attention appeared to be concentrated on restoring the situation. Commander Robertson had been roused from slumber by a signalman with a copy of the fatal message, and had gone straight up to the plotting-room on the Admiral's bridge. The Admiral and Commodore Brind were already in consultation there, and the atmosphere which Robertson sensed when he joined them was one of intensified resolution. If it had been necessary to sink the *Bismarck* before the catastrophe of the *Hood's* destruction, it was doubly necessary after it.

When, the evening before, the Commander-in-Chief had heard of the *Bismarck* being sighted in the Denmark Strait, he had been 550 miles of the south-eastward of her. Examining at that time the plotted positions of the *Bismarck* and the various British squadrons on the chart, Sir John had reckoned that if the *Bismarck* continued on through the Denmark Strait, a meeting between her and the *Hood's* squadron was almost certain in the morning. When that meeting took place, Sir John went on to argue, one of three things was likely to happen. An action might be fought. If so, there was no certainty that the *Bismarck* would be sunk, or even that she would not do more damage than she received. But he hoped that at the least she would be slowed down enough to enable him to come up and finish her off. But on sighting the *Hood's* squadron, the *Bismarck* might decide to avoid action. In which direction she would endeavour to escape in that case depended on the relative position of the *Hood's* squadron when the *Bismarck* first saw it. If it was approaching her from the southward, she would probably turn back into the Denmark Strait and make for Norway by the north of Iceland. But if the *Hood* was to the westward, then there would be a chance for the *Bismarck* to break away to the southward or south-eastward, either to return to the North Sea south of Iceland or to continue on her enterprise. Viewing these alternatives of the situation, and taking into consideration his own force's present position, Sir John Tovey had decided that the best move for him was to cover the two contingencies of an enemy retreat back through the Denmark Strait or an attempted break-away to the southward or south-eastward. Accordingly, he altered course slightly to the northward to make for a position which he calculated would be about right for the purpose he had in mind.

Unfortunately, instead of turning back for Germany or being either sunk or fought to something like a standstill by Vice-Admiral Holland's squadron, the *Bismarck* had administered a swift defeat to that squadron and had continued on her south-westerly way apparently unscathed. The unhappy result was that she was now well in advance of the Commander-in-Chief's squadron, and the latter's chances of getting within reach of her looked very unpromising, so long as she continued on her present south-westerly course. The question was, how long was she likely to do so?

As matters now stood, there seemed to be three possible courses of action for the enemy ships to follow. They might be making for a rendezvous with an oiler, whence, with their tanks replenished, they would issue forth to prey on shipping, afterwards returning to the same or another rendezvous for further fuel supplies. Though there was a wide range of possibility regarding the location of these rendezvous, Admiral Tovey had two main areas in mind. One was the West Greenland coast, adjoining the Davis Strait, where there were many inlets and anchorages suitable for use by raiding warships. Alternatively, the Admiral thought the enemy ships might go south to where the weather was fine enough for an ocean rendezvous to be used; say in the region of the Azores or the Canaries.

There had, indeed, been intelligence reports of German oilers in these southerly latitudes.

If the enemy were bound for the Davis Strait, he would probably continue in his present direction till nightfall, when he would be just about clear for rounding Cape Farewell, and would then endeavour to shake off his shadowers preparatory to turning north-west. But if he were going south, it was hard to estimate at this stage how he would act. Of course, the *Bismarck* would only be making for a rendezvous with an oiler if she were substantially undamaged. About this, however, Sir John Tovey had as yet[1] no information. The early news of the action with the *Hood* and *Prince of Wales* had referred to the loss and damage to the British ships and had been silent about the enemy: and it was upon this negative evidence that Sir John had initially to make up his mind about what to do next.

If the *Bismarck* were, however, damaged to an extent that called for early repairs, she was probably intending to make for a dockyard. If so, she might be thinking of a French Atlantic yard, presumably either Brest or St. Nazaire or even Dakar, or a French (Toulon) or Italian yard in the Mediterranean; or perhaps a Spanish yard, in which case it would probably be Ferrol. The direct course from the *Bismarck's* present position to any of these ports was well to the east of south, whereas she was still steering south-west. To reach a dockyard, she would sooner or later, therefore, have to make a large turn to port, and the farther she continued out into the Atlantic, the bigger the eventual turn to port would have to be: though it might be made by a gradual semicircular sweep rather than by an abrupt alteration. This was the second possibility.

The third was in part a variant of the second, and lay in a return to Germany for repairs in the greater security of the Baltic. But there was a further reason, independent of action damage, for a return to the Fatherland. From a political point of view, a return home appeared by no means improbable. The *Bismarck* had just won a very notable success against the British surface Navy. If she went back now, she could be received as

[1] This survey of the situation was taking place between 7 a.m. and 8 a.m.

the homecoming victor, and Doctor Goebbels's propaganda machine could be trusted to make the most of the situation.

Which of these three possibilities was the most likely one? There was no certain indication, and the choice was mainly a matter of guesswork. If the *Bismarck's* destination were the Davis Strait, Sir John was very unfavourably placed to bring her to action, since she was already well ahead of him for that direction. In that case, he could do little more than follow her westward, if necessary taking his force to Newfoundland for fuel. He was, however, naturally reluctant to cross the Atlantic, since this would put the *Bismarck* on interior lines, at all events for a time.

If, on the other hand, the *Bismarck* were making for a French, Spanish or Italian port, everything depended on how soon she turned to port for her destination. Were she to make a wide enough detour, she might be able to outrun pursuit; because the British forces, having to make a double journey, out and back, against her single one out, might well have to abandon the chase and return home before she was compelled to steer south-east or east for her port of arrival. But if she turned to port soon enough, Sir John Tovey, being then on interior lines himself, might be able to cut a corner and intercept her.

Even so, interception was none too certain unless Sir John Tovey took ground to the southward by anticipating the *Bismarck's* possible alteration of course to port. The Commander-in-Chief was almost as far north as the *Bismarck* herself, and if he was to make sure of cutting her off on the way to the Straits of Gibraltar or the Bay of Biscay he needed to get further down that way in good time. To do this, however, was to endanger interception if the *Bismarck* turned back for Germany. To cover this latter contingency, Sir John required to remain well north, and the further he went south the more he opened the way for a German escape back into the North Sea.

What was Sir John to do? Was he to gamble on the *Bismarck* following one particular course of action, and accept the certainty that if she followed one of the others she would get clear away? Or was he to take the compromise line of endeavouring to counter all three courses, with the knowledge that his chances of countering any particular one were none too good? He decided that there was insufficient evidence of the enemy's ultimate intentions to justify a gamble, and that a mean course that would give some, even if not a good, opportunity of dealing with any enemy move was the best in the circumstances.

Moreover, when in doubt, as he reminded himself, it was necessary to keep in mind that a westerly break-out was still the most dangerous enemy course and required to be given priority in the British dispositions. As a bold alteration southward by the Home Fleet would disregard this priority and would also lay open the way back to Germany, Sir John determined against it. He would, instead, content himself with steering to close the enemy so far as was possible on the present bearing. Just after 8 a.m. he accordingly altered course 20 degrees to port to the most favourable closing course; and nearly three hours later, at 10.50 a.m., he came round another 20 degrees in the same direction, as the enemy was found to have been edging round to the southward, too, following the curve of the eastern Greenland coast.

Meanwhile, the calamitous news of the early morning had given rise to intense activity among the Naval Staff in the Admiralty. In the early morning, Captain R. A. B. Edwards, the Director of Operations (Home) had been met by a grave-faced Duty Captain with a copy of Rear-Admiral Wake-Walker's signal that '*Hood* has blown up'. There were three people to be acquainted with an event of this gravity at once, all of whom were sleeping in the Admiralty building, so that within a few minutes all were assembled in the War Room. These were, in ascending order, Rear-Admiral A. J. Power, the Assistant Chief of the Naval Staff (Home), Vice-Admiral Sir Tom Phillips, Vice-Chief of the Naval Staff, and Admiral Sir Dudley Pound, the First Sea Lord and Chief of the Naval Staff. Of these three, Rear-Admiral Power was only responsible for operations in Home Waters, which included the Atlantic, and could therefore, together with Captain Edwards (also concerned only with Home Waters), give his whole attention to the *Bismarck* affair. Sir

The Admiralty Takes Some Vigorous Steps

Dudley Pound and Sir Tom Phillips, on the other hand, were responsible for naval operations everywhere in the world, and since the German invasion of Crete was at this time in progress, they could not devote themselves exclusively to the *Bismarck's* escape. Nevertheless, the latter was obviously a matter of the highest importance and both officers necessarily kept in very close touch with what was going on in the Atlantic, Sir Tom Phillips especially. It is said of him that at this period he never left the War Room except to eat and sleep, and the Admiralty building not at all.[1]

There were two others who also took a keen interest in the *Bismarck* proceedings, and for whom the loss of the *Hood* had political as well as strategical implications. One, Mr. A. V. Alexander, was First Lord of the Admiralty, and though not a member of the War Cabinet was the political head of the Navy. The second was the Prime Minister and Minister of Defence, Mr. Winston Churchill. They, however, were not present in the War Room on this occasion.

To the heads of the Naval Staff, the repulse of the first British intercepting force with the loss of so famous a ship as the *Hood* was a heavy blow. They met it in almost identically the same spirit as Sir John Tovey was displaying at this same moment in his flagship out in the Atlantic. It was now more essential than ever for the *Bismarck* to be overtaken and destroyed, and every available resource must be brought into use to this end.

Not that the present crisis had caught the Admiralty unawares. When the emergence of the *Bismarck* from the Baltic had first been rumoured, the Operations Staff[2] had begun to take careful stock of the naval forces in the possible strategic area, and the general state of affairs in this and other relevant respects was therefore already in their minds. From the first report of her sailing, there had been a shifting of units to meet the developing situation. It will be recalled that as early as May 21st, before the *Hood's* squadron had left Scapa, the *Victorious* had been trans-

---

[1] These senior officers were, of course, assisted by many junior officers in the various divisions of the naval staff.

[2] A term which can be said to include all or any of the naval officers mentioned above as well as their unnamed subordinates.

ferred to Sir John Tovey's command and the *Repulse* had been ordered north from the Clyde to join his flag. Both these ships had been intended as the heavy escort for troop convoy WS8B, due to sail for the Middle East via the Cape. The convoy's sailing was not delayed in consequence of this removal of its big-ship protection, but it put to sea as previously arranged on May 22nd, accompanied by its cruiser and destroyer escort only.

There were at this time, ten other convoys at sea in the Atlantic, some of which had battleship or cruiser escort, while others had only a screen of lighter vessels, destroyers, frigates, corvettes or sloops. Of all these various escorting ships, only the battleships, cruisers, and fleet destroyers could be regarded as having any battle value against the *Bismarck*. These classes could, however, be considered as a potential reserve to be brought in against her, provided she came within reach of them and provided the risk of removing them from their convoys was acceptable.

In addition to this reserve of warships actually at sea, there were forces in harbour which might also play a useful role, either for direct combat purposes or as 'replace' ships for convoy escorts summoned away from convoy duty. Of these forces, the most important was Vice-Admiral Sir James Somerville's Force H at Gibraltar, consisting of the battle cruiser *Renown* (sister ship to the *Repulse*), the aircraft carrier *Ark Royal*, the cruiser *Sheffield*, and six destroyers. Force H's normal duty was to seal the western exit of the Mediterranean against the Italian Fleet, and hitherto all its activities had been inside the Mediterranean. But with its seagoing mobility, the Force was equally available at a moment's notice for operations in the Atlantic.

Thousands of miles away on the other side of the ocean, there was another capital ship, H.M.S. *Revenge*, lying in Halifax harbour, Nova Scotia. She was certainly a long way off, but the Naval Staff at the Admiralty had nevertheless marked her down early in the proceedings as a ship that might come in handy, especially in case the *Bismarck* made for the American side of the Atlantic.

The transfer of the *Repulse* and *Victorious* from Convoy

The Admiralty Takes Some Vigorous Steps

WS8B to Sir John Tovey's command had been the only modification initially made to pre-arranged dispositions. On receiving the news, however, of the *Bismarck* being sighted in the Denmark Strait on the evening of the 23rd, the Admiralty took another step. Now that the enemy battleship was obviously making a bid to get away into the Atlantic, it was felt that since Convoy WS8B was a troop convoy some action was imperative to compensate for the withdrawal of its big-ship escort. Accordingly, within two hours of the sighting report coming through, a wireless message was despatched to Sir James Somerville to raise steam for full speed and to start bringing his force to the northward at once with the object of covering the convoy. This signal left the Admiralty about 10 p.m. on the 23rd, and at 2 a.m. the ships of Force H were on their way out of Gibraltar harbour. Four hours later, when the *Hood* blew up, they were about halfway between Capes Trafalgar and St. Vincent, well out at sea.

The disastrous outcome of the *Hood–Bismarck* engagement spurred the Admiralty on to further and more drastic action. The situation had changed a great deal for the worse, and every possible step that could in any way contribute to the enemy's destruction would have to be taken. The idea of sending Force H to cover Convoy WS8B was abandoned and it was decided instead to bring that Force in against the *Bismarck* herself.

This was one of the earliest of a succession of orders, instructions, and information signals sent out by the Admiralty in the process of organizing the greatest possible concentration of force against the German ships. A couple of hundred miles ahead of Force H, the cruiser *London* (Captain R. M. Servaes) was escorting a convoy from Gibraltar to the United Kingdom. She was ordered to leave her convoy and proceed towards a position 55° N., 35° W., to intercept the *Bismarck* and shadow. She increased speed and went off north-west as directed.[1] Down near the Azores, the cruiser *Edinburgh* (Commodore C. M.

---

[1] Some hours later, these orders were revoked and the Admiralty ordered *London* to go south to search for enemy oilers south of the Azores. They were eventually found and sunk.

Blackman) had been patrolling for German blockade runners and supply tankers for a number of days. Commodore Blackman had just intercepted a German merchant ship and taken prisoners on board when he head the news of the *Bismarck* being sighted. He at once set off north-westerly to intercept, on the assumption that the *Bismarck* would come south-west to where he thought she might have supply ships waiting for her. This action he took on his own initiative. A few hours after the *Hood's* destruction, when he was about 600 miles west of Cape Finisterre, he received a signal from the Admiralty to proceed as necessary for intercepting and shadowing, without regard to fuel consumption. An oiler, he was told, would be sent to replenish him if he ran out of fuel. The prospect of the *Edinburgh* lying helplessly motionless in submarine waters, with the *Bismarck* and *Prinz Eugen* also at large, while an oiler tried to find her, was somewhat startling: but Commodore Blackman increased speed to 25 knots.

Hundreds of miles to the north-west, the battleship *Ramillies* (Captain A. D. Read, R.N.) was with Convoy HX127 in mid-Atlantic. She, too, was ordered away from her convoy to close and intercept the enemy from the westward. As was usual when with a convoy, the *Ramillies* had been steaming at 8 knots. Captain Read rang down for 18 knots, but his twenty-seven-year-old ship took some little time to work up to this speed and in the process unavoidably emitted volumes of black funnel smoke. Captain Read felt very awkward about this, since he had made a number of reproving signals during the previous days to various merchant ships of the convoy for doing the same thing, and he felt that the Masters must now be enjoying themselves. In half an hour, he had left the convoy behind and was steering north-north-west to get to the westward of the *Bismarck*.

At the moment she was, as he knew from the *Norfolk's* and *Suffolk's* reports, coming almost straight towards him. In his opinion, she was making for the South Atlantic; and if so, he ought easily to be able to reach an intercepting position. But even if he could, Captain Read doubted, in view of the *Bismarck's* much higher speed, whether the *Ramillies* would be able to bring her to action if she were disinclined for it. He might, however, be able to head her off for a short period, which might possibly allow some of the other hunting forces to gain ground. Later in the day, the Admiralty sent him a signal not to become engaged with the *Bismarck* unless the latter were in action with other British forces. This was a counsel of impossibility—unless the *Ramillies* were to give up the attempt at interception altogether. For if she were to sight the *Bismarck* when the latter was not engaged with other British forces, the decision to seek or avoid action would not rest with the *Ramillies*, owing to her unfavourable margin of speed.

Still farther to the westward, the battleship *Revenge* had been told to raise steam and proceed to sea from Halifax. She was to come east to take over the convoy HX127 that the *Ramillies* had just left.

Back on the eastern side of the ocean, about 500 miles from the Irish coast, the battleship *Rodney* (Captain F. H. G. Dalrymple-Hamilton, R.N.) with the destroyers *Somali*, *Mashona*, *Tartar* and *Eskimo* were escorting the *Britannic* en route to the United States. They had left the Clyde at 1 p.m. on May 22nd, the *Rodney* being due to refit at Boston, U.S.A., on arrival in America. She had on board as passengers, Captain C. Coppinger, R.N., three Midshipmen doing their first sea trip, and Lieutenant-Commander Wellings, U.S.N., together with some twenty other officers and 500 ratings, including invalids for Canada, some suffering from shell shock. On the upper deck were secured many cases of refitting stores and on the boat deck were two very large wooden cases containing two eight-barrel pom-pom mountings which gave the ship something of the appearance of a Norwegian timber vessel. Of her prospective overhaul, the *Rodney* was in the most urgent need. She had not been properly refitted for over two years, and her machinery was in a most precarious condition. One engine-room had broken down twice during the previous month, leaving only one propeller on which to return to harbour, and the boilers were in a similarly shaky state. She was to show what an invalid ship could do in an emergency.

When the *Bismarck* had been first sighted by the *Suffolk* on May 23rd, she was about 800 miles north-north-west from the *Rodney*. As the shadowing reports came through, it became clear to Captain Dalrymple-Hamilton that the enemy was quite likely to be coming south, and that, if so, the *Rodney* might very well be able to gain an intercepting position. But he thought nevertheless there was only a small chance of the *Bismarck* surviving the attentions of the Home Fleet long enough for her to come within *Rodney's* reach. However, the westerly course being steered to take the *Britannic* to America could not be improved upon as an intercepting course against the *Bismarck*, and so Captain Dalrymple-Hamilton went on as he was.

Next morning, when the sinking of the *Hood* came through, he realized that his ship might now play a larger part in the operations than he had at first thought. He then formed an Operations Committee, consisting of Captain Coppinger, the Commander and Navigating Officer of the *Rodney*, and Lieutenant-Commander Wellings, which subsequently met in the charthouse to discuss each phase of the operation and to advise on what action should be taken in regard to the various signals that came in and events that occurred.

It was not unexpected on board when, shortly before noon on the 24th, a signal came through from the Admiralty for the *Rodney* to leave one destroyer with the *Britannic* and, with the others, to steer an intercepting course for the *Bismarck*. As the *Rodney* was already steering it, she went on as before, increasing speed and taking the *Somali*, *Tartar* and *Mashona* with her.

Thus within six hours of the *Hood's* destruction, two additional battleships, one battle cruiser, one aircraft carrier, three cruisers and nine destroyers had joined directly in the chase. A concentration was thus being arranged which for the vastness of the area involved and for its dramatic character had few, if any, rivals. In some respects, and particularly in geographical extent, the Trafalgar campaign was not dissimilar, as Captain Phillips of the *Norfolk* remarked to his Admiral at the time. But Lord Barham and his fellow Sea Lords of 1805 had had no wireless to prolong their immediate control of operations be-

The Admiralty Takes Some Vigorous Steps

yond the seashore. In 1941, the responsible officers at the Admiralty were able to pull invisible strings which, within a few minutes, could bring far distant and widely separated warships swinging round under full rudder to converge from half a dozen different directions on the estimated position of the enemy squadron. This impressive concentration of force, covering more than a million square miles of ocean and involving the ships of three or four different commands, was necessarily being initiated by the Admiralty because only the Admiralty possessed the combination of information and authority to order it.

CHAPTER 5

The Shadowing Goes On

The *Norfolk* and *Suffolk* had automatically gone on shadowing after the dawn battle as they had been doing before. The *Suffolk* was again following from fine on the starboard quarter, this time assisted by the oily wake the *Bismarck* was leaving behind her; while the *Norfolk* was once more out on the port quarter, with the *Prince of Wales* on her quarter again. The previous string of enemy reports was continued, the two cruisers each sending out signals of the enemy's position, course and speed about every twenty minutes during the periods when they were severally in contact. Overhead until about 9 a.m. was the Sunderland flying boat Z /201; and shortly after she went back, a Hudson, M /269, arrived on the scene from Iceland.

For some hours, the weather was clear all round the horizon and the task of shadowing therefore comparatively simple. The cruisers kept the enemy ships in sight at fifteen to eighteen miles' distance and were able to conform to their movements without much difficulty, even though the Germans kept making large alterations of course to one side or the other in the evident endeavour to shake off their trackers.

About 11 a.m., however, banks of mist were sighted ahead, and soon the shadowers were contending with the same treacherous and uncertain weather conditions as they had experienced on the previous night, the visibility again varying between seventeen or eighteen miles and two or three. Both cruisers closed in as much as they dared, but about noon they one after the other lost sight of the enemy in mist and drizzle.

Three hundred miles to the eastward, the Commander-in-Chief was pushing on after the enemy at his squadron's best speed. It has already been described how Sir John Tovey was steering a mean course chosen with a view to competing with any of the three possible enemy courses of action; namely, raiding operations based either on Greenland or somewhere in the south, passage on to an Atlantic or Mediterranean dockyard, or a return to Germany. For the time being, the enemy's onward choice of direction was somewhat restricted by the coast of Greenland, his present course of south-west being necessary to take him clear of Cape Farewell. After he had passed it, he would be free to alter course to the westward or north-westward if he so desired. Sir John Tovey's course was a little inwards, about west-south-west, making him close very slowly on the enemy along the relative line east to west. But there was no way of closing more rapidly at present.

As the time passed, the Admiral's Chief of Staff, Commodore Brind, became a little uneasy about the British pursuit plan. He had not altogether agreed with the Admiral's original reasoning which had led to the compromise course now being steered. The Commodore feared that this course might be injudicious in that it tried to do too much, and that the endeavour to cover all enemy movements could result in covering none. He felt that it would be better to make some choice of probabilities in order to put more money on the more likely eventuality at the expense of the less.

As in duty bound, he made his uneasiness known to his Chief. He urged that the endeavour to allow for the *Bismarck* doubling back might well prevent a contact if she should continue onward. He pointed out that the one certain piece of information was that she had so far consistently maintained a south-westerly course and that each hour she continued on it made a double back less likely. The Commodore therefore favoured an early alteration to the southward by the *King George V's* squadron to make more allowance for what he believed to be the more probable enemy intention.

82

The Admiral, however, rejected this suggestion. In the process of making up his mind, he would naturally hear any views that his staff had to offer. Indeed, Sir John always encouraged them to speak their minds quite freely. But the final responsibility was his; and if, after all had been said, he thought differently to some or even all of his staff, it was his duty to follow his own judgment. Sir John maintained the course of the fleet.

To the ships in company with him it seemed a very long and weary time as they raced onwards in dirty weather at 27 knots, while the plots gave no immediate promise of an action. Captain Bovell of the *Victorious* found station-keeping at such high speed distinctly trying. Of the watch-keeping abilities of his officers of the watch he was entirely ignorant, and this was a time when one small error of judgment might easily cause a disastrous collision. The *Victorious* had four knots in hand, but the *Repulse* astern of her was fully extended and, not wanting to reduce her revolutions, was constantly riding up unpleasantly close on the *Victorious's* quarter. Down below, the Engine-Commander (Engineer-Commander Ward), with a raw engine-room complement, many of them 'hostilities only' men who had never before been to sea, was having almost as difficult a time as his Captain on the bridge.

The *Norfolk* had lost sight of the *Bismarck* at 11.50 a.m. Owing to the latter's reduction of speed, the *Norfolk* had been gaining bearing on her and was only about 20 degrees abaft her beam when drizzling rain had obscured the *Bismarck* from view. The *Norfolk* continued to steam along out of touch with the enemy in low visibility. This was nothing new; she had done this for long periods already. But now Rear-Admiral Wake-Walker was uneasy. With the *Norfolk* placed as she was, the *Bismarck* would come very close to her if she (the *Bismarck*) altered course a certain amount to port. And in this weather the Norfolk would get no warning of the *Bismarck's* approach till she came in sight at point-blank range, since the *Norfolk's* radar was not operative along the enemy's probable present bearing. There was no special reason why the enemy should turn to port at this particular time. Nevertheless, the Rear-Admiral had a curious sense of impending danger and he decided to drop bearing. Just before 12.30 p.m. he turned to Captain Phillips and said: 'I have a feeling the *Bismarck* is uncomfortably close on our beam. Alter course 360 degrees to port.' The *Norfolk* swung round through a whole circle, thereby dropping back about three to four miles on the enemy relative to the previous line of advance, and came back to her course.

Forty minutes later, the visibility lengthened somewhat and the *Bismarck* came in sight on the *Norfolk's* bow and only eight miles off. Her course, moreover, was 180 degrees, which meant that she had, in fact, altered course 30 degrees to port since last seen; and a subsequent plot back of her movements indicated that she had made her alteration at 12.40 p.m., or only a few minutes after Rear-Admiral Wake-Walker had decided to circle to port. Had he not had the intuition to do so, what he feared would probably have happened. The *Norfolk* and *Bismarck* would have converged unseen until they sighted each other through the mist, when the *Norfolk* must have been blown out of the water. Even as it was, the enemy was dangerously close, and the *Norfolk* sheered away until she was again obscured. She sighted the enemy again for a short time at 2.35 p.m., and at 3.15 p.m. when the visibility increased and the enemy was seen at seventeen miles.

The enemy's alteration of course, being made inside the cover of mist, seems to have caused the *Suffolk* temporarily to lose contact. She soon, however, began to pick up the *Norfolk's* signals based on visual sightings and by their aid was able to follow round. By ten minutes past four, the *Suffolk* was again in radar touch and was resuming her reports.

Before 5 p.m., more mist had appeared and the *Norfolk*, in turn, lost touch with the enemy. But, by this time, the *Suffolk* had him firmly held by radar and so was able to keep her blinded colleague informed of the enemy's movements. Thus did science and human eyesight supplement and reinforce each other in keeping continuous track of the escaping enemy ships. Sometimes ordinary vision failed and sometimes radar contact. On several occasions the one filled in the blanks left by the other.

But it was the *Suffolk's* radar which played the major part in keeping hold of the enemy in such adverse weather; and indeed both Rear-Admiral Wake-Walker and Captain Phillips were frequently blessing her new radar set, while lamenting that the *Norfolk* did not have it too. The successful continuance of the shadowing also demonstrated the soundness of the dispositions employed, with one ship on either quarter of the chase. Thus stationed, an enemy alteration of course which might take her away from one shadower was bound to bring her closer to the other, whose reports should then tell the first one what had happened.

During the early afternoon, the Hudson M/269 had returned to base: but she was almost immediately replaced by a Catalina, G/210, which had left Iceland at 9.15 a.m. But after two hours (at 4.40 p.m.), this latter developed engine trouble and had to return. No more air contacts were made during the day. One thing the Catalina was able to do was to give the Rear-Admiral a visual link with the *Suffolk*, who he learnt was twenty-six miles from the *Norfolk* and fifteen miles astern of the enemy.

The news that the enemy had altered course to south brought Sir John Tovey considerable relief. The uncertainty as to the enemy's intentions during the previous six or seven hours had made them very anxious ones, especially in regard to the competing claims of a return to Germany and a continuance of the outward voyage.[1] The enemy's alteration to the southward did not remove the Greenland possibility from the Admiral's mind. Indeed, he thought the alteration might well be a ruse to mislead the shadowing ships before the enemy turned north-west after dark. It did, however, seem to make a return to Germany a little less likely. But it also occurred to Sir John that the enemy's southerly course might be for the purpose of leading the British shadowers towards a concentration of U-boats. Even if the fog of

---

[1] Sir John Tovey's decision that he could not afford to ignore during this period the possibility of an enemy double-back towards Germany was soundly based. It became known afterwards that there had been a hot and prolonged argument between the German Admiral Lutjens in the *Bismarck* and the Captain of the ship, Lindemann, the latter arguing strongly for a return to Germany, the Admiral insisting on a continuance westward.

war had been rendered a little less dense, it was still thick enough.

What, however, made the southerly alteration by the *Bismarck* so very welcome was the increased chance of interception that it offered. The Admiral's possible rate of closing on the enemy was now much increased, and as long as the *Bismarck* continued this course the distance between her and the *King George V* could be promisingly shortened. Indeed, if she went on with it all night, a contact would be possible about 9 a.m. the next morning. That the enemy was being so obliging suggested that he might be ignorant of the presence of the *King George V's* squadron. He might indeed be mistaking the *Prince of Wales* for the *King George V.*[1]

So far, so good. But Sir John Tovey was worried about the possibility of an attempt by the *Bismarck* to escape from observation by the use of high speed during the night. If she put on a sudden spurt she might give her shadowers the slip before they had realized what was happening. It was to be assumed that she could do this. Sir John knew about the oily wake she was leaving behind her, but he was not inclined to attach overmuch importance to it. Oil spreads out quickly on the sea surface and a very small leak can make a broad oil track. It was necessary to credit the *Bismarck* with having still her normal full speed available on demand and as therefore being capable of an increase of 7 or 8 knots whenever she chose. If she waited till after dark, she would have the best opportunity of making this increase without being seen and so of gaining a lead on her pursuers which might well result in their losing contact for good. If she was mistaking the *Prince of Wales* for the *King George V*, and was therefore unaware of the Commander-in-Chief's squadron being out after her, she would not mind proceeding at only moderate speed during daylight.

It was this contingency of which Sir John Tovey was chiefly apprehensive during the afternoon hours while he was considering the effects of the *Bismarck's* southerly turn; and the feeling grew with him that he must find means of slowing the *Bismarck* up before darkness set in. There was only one present way of

---

[1] He was, in fact, making this very mistake.

86

doing this—an attack by the *Victorious'* aircraft. While the enemy had been steering south-west, he had been beyond the range of those aircraft. But his southerly turn had at last brought him within reach of them. Just within reach: but just should be enough. If they could only get some torpedoes into her and so inflict underwater damage, they might reduce her speed sufficiently to scotch any inconvenient spurts during the night. The Admiral had some time before asked the *Victorious* from what range she could launch an attack, and Captain Bovell had replied one hundred miles, provided his carrier could continue to close the enemy while the aircraft were away, so that they would have a shorter distance to return. The *Victorious* was not at the moment within 100 miles of the *Bismarck*: but she could get there by about 9 p.m., though at the expense of losing some bearing on the enemy, which might mean that she would not be available for search or other operations against the enemy next day.

Sir John Tovey had to take this into account in considering whether to send her off now, and had also to bear in mind that most of her air crews were untrained for sea work and therefore necessarily inexpert. However, he had known about their lack of carrier training when he had decided to take the *Victorious* with him in the first place, and this was no time to dwell on possible inefficiency. He believed the Swordfish were well led and he knew they would all do their best.

The question of whether to use them now or reserve them for another occasion caused him no difficulty. The prevention of a high-speed escape by the enemy under cover of darkness was what was weighing most with him : and shortly before 3 p.m. he signalled that the *Victorious,* escorted by the 2nd Cruiser Squadron under Vice-Admiral A. T. B. Curteis, was to close the *Bismarck* and fly off to the attack when within 100 miles. A few minutes later, he turned the *King George V* and *Repulse* 40 degrees to port to a course of 200 degrees. This was 20 degrees inwards to the *Bismarck's* course, and gave the best closing rate that could be managed without losing bearing (i.e. dropping gradually astern of the enemy).

The Shadowing Goes On

The *Victorious* turned out of the line, and she and the four cruisers began to open out to starboard. With no risk from hostile air attack, the *Victorious'* aircraft could be ranged in plenty of time and there was ample opportunity for discussion with the Squadron Commander and the pilots. The weather was getting worse, and Captain Bovell had grave doubts whether any of the pilots, untrained as many of them were, would be able to land on after the attack. He hoped, however, that they would at least be able to save themselves, even though they crashed their aircraft. He noted with satisfaction that the squadron leader, Esmonde, was full of confidence that all would go well, and under his leadership the whole squadron were so keen and enthusiastic that it was difficult to think they would not succeed.

With so small a torpedo squadron, it was clear that all the Swordfish must attack and that none could be spared for shadowing or reconnaissance: and as the decisive target was the *Bismarck* and not the *Prinz Eugen*, it was equally clear they must all attack the former. Captain Bovell proposed, however, to use his Fulmars two at a time for shadowing, in the hope that a second attack could be sent in.

To the westward, Rear-Admiral Wake-Walker's shadowing vessels were still holding on to the enemy in very variable weather, sometimes clear and sometimes thick. Just before 4 p.m., the Rear-Admiral received a signal from the Admiralty which caused him a certain amount of perplexity and some concern. This signal requested his intentions as regards the *Prince of Wales* re-engaging. How was this signal to be interpreted? Was it meant as a plain and unqualified inquiry? Or was it a gentle hint that the Admiralty thought he was being insufficiently pugnacious and that he should have sought an action by this time? It was impossible to tell. The signal might contain an implied reproof or it might not. The possibility that it might worried him rather, and not unnaturally. Every officer is particularly sensitive to even the faintest suggestion that his ardour for battle may be in any degree lacking. It was now ten hours since the *Hood's* destruction had put the *Prince of Wales* at the Rear-

Admiral's disposal, and if he had not sent her to re-engage during this fairly long interval, why did the Admiralty now ask him if he meant to do so unless they sought to indicate that he should have done it? The Rear-Admiral took some time in writing a reply to this signal, tearing up a number of draft answers before he was satisfied. Eventually, he despatched one which said that he considered the *Prince of Wales* should not re-engage until other heavy ships were in contact or unless interception failed. It was, he added, doubtful whether the *Prince of Wales* had enough speed to compel an action. The Admiralty made no comment, and three hours later there came a personal message from the First Sea Lord to *Norfolk* and *Suffolk* saying that their shadowing had been admirable. He told them to keep it up and wished them good luck. Nevertheless, Rear-Admiral Wake-Walker would have preferred that the earlier signal had not been made.

Sir John Tovey had read the Admiralty's signal to the Rear-Admiral with disfavour. He was quite satisfied with the latter's conduct in continuing the pursuit without endeavouring to bring on an action, and Sir John was slightly alarmed at what he thought might be the Admiralty's intention to push the Rear-Admiral into seeking an engagement (if he could). Sir John had no confidence that such an engagement would have a satisfactory outcome and he feared it might well result in the cruisers being damaged and contact being lost. He therefore made up his mind that, should the Admiralty persist, he would intervene and make his opinion known. He naturally did not want to do this, if he could avoid it; since it was obviously most undesirable that he should publicly contest the Admiralty's exhortations, instructions, or orders, whichever form they might take. Nor did he wish to break wireless silence for this purpose. But he would do it if necessary.

At intervals during the day, the Admiralty had been sending out situation reports for the information of the seagoing forces. They told all ships where the enemy was believed to be, based on the shadowing ships' signals, and what orders had been given to the various British units that had been or were being brought into the hunt; also in what positions the different British hunting forces were estimated to be from time to time. Most of the sea-going officers have testified to the great value of these Admiralty summaries of the situation; and they certainly gave a series of very clear and useful pictures of what was happening, so far as the Admiralty knew it. Without these Admiralty summaries, it would have been difficult for technical reasons for some of the ships to know what orders were being sent to the others. But how these latter would interpret their orders was often a matter of guesswork; and there was, as will be seen later, a certain danger in the Admiralty doing the guessing.

There was also the risk in such broadcast reports that if the enemy were able to decipher them, they gave him in ideally convenient form the very information he would most want to have. It is to be presumed that the Admiralty had at this time sufficient reason to believe that the deciphering of these signals was a danger that could be safely ignored.[1]

By the late afternoon, Rear-Admiral Wake-Walker had begun to evolve a plan in his mind for luring the *Bismarck* over towards the Commander-in-Chief. The *Bismarck* was proceeding at well below her full speed. The *Norfolk* and *Prince of Wales* should therefore close up on her and engage her from the port quarter. If the *Bismarck* accepted this challenge and joined action, the *Norfolk* and *Prince of Wales* would then retire to the eastward in the hope of drawing the enemy after them towards the *King George V's* squadron. Whether this plan would have succeeded remains an open question, because the enemy acted first.

Ever since the onset of misty conditions, Captain Ellis of the *Suffolk* had been expecting that the *Bismarck* might endeavour to round on one or other of the shadowers under cover of low visibility and trap them at close range. At about 6.30 p.m., the enemy, being about 26,000 yards ahead of the *Suffolk*, disappeared into a fog-bank. Captain Ellis had been resting his radar during a clear patch, but when the enemy ships were lost to sight he brought it again into action. It was just as well that he

---

[1] The author has been informed by German officers that British signals could not be deciphered at this time.

did, for the radar began to report the range as quickly decreasing. When it was down to 22,000 yards, Captain Ellis, on the alert against an ambush, put his wheel over for a turn to port and increased to full speed. As the *Suffolk* swung round under helm, the *Bismarck* appeared out of the mist ahead at a range of 20,000 yards and opened fire with all her guns. Captain Ellis immediately ordered funnel smoke to be made, but before the ship had got under cover of this screen, the enemy had fired nine salvoes and some more came down in the smoke. By great good fortune, the enemy's initial salvoes were a long way out—at least 1,000 yards short and out for line—and by the time they were getting dangerously close, the *Suffolk's* pall of smoke was streaming out and she was hidden by it.

This brief action took both ships over towards the *Norfolk* and *Prince of Wales*, the latter of whom opened fire in support of the *Suffolk* as the battle came her way. Her range from the enemy was, however, very long—about 30,000 yards—and though she fired a number of salvoes, it is doubtful if her shooting was effective. The *Bismarck* in any case was clearly in no mood for an action with a heavy ship. She hauled off and made away to the westward at high speed.[1]

The *Suffolk* herself had naturally opened fire, and as she turned away to open the range from the *Bismarck*, her guns came round more and more on to an after bearing until the foremost turrets at high elevation had their muzzles pointing unpleasantly close to the bridge. As one of their salvoes went off there was a crash of glass as all the bridge windows were blown in. Since there were no wind baffles nor other weather protection once the windows had gone, the Captain and others of the bridge personnel soon began to feel the effects of exposure to the bitter wind that was now sweeping unimpeded through the bridge.[2]

[1] This turn westward by the *Bismarck* is interesting as showing her probable reaction to any previous attempt by the Rear-Admiral to re-engage.

[2] The *Norfolk* had then an open bridge which was, however, comparatively draughtless by virtue of good wind baffles. The author understands that the fitting of the new radar set in the *Suffolk* interfered with her wind baffles, so that when the glass screens were broken there was no alternative protection such as the *Norfolk* had.

The Shadowing Goes On

Unhappily, the *Bismarck's* retreat to the westward put a spoke in Rear-Admiral Wake-Walker's hopes of decoying her east. Instead of the *Norfolk* and *Prince of Wales* turning away to lead the *Bismarck* in that direction, it was she who had made off in the opposite one. The interception problem was thereby rendered worse and not better.[1]

This episode had brought all three of the British shadowing ships into fairly close proximity, and for some reason Rear-Admiral Wake-Walker decided he would keep them together and place them all on the enemy's port side. He therefore stationed them in a rough line ahead, the *Suffolk* leading because of her superior radar capabilities, the *Prince of Wales* following her, and the *Norfolk* bringing up the rear.

The enemy's westward retirement had adversely affected the *Victorious'* approach problem by lengthening the distance she would have to go. Instead of her reaching the 100 mile circle from the *Bismarck* at about 9 p.m. as previously expected, she was still 120 miles away an hour later. As the rate of closing on the *Bismarck* was very slow and as the weather was still deteriorating, Captain Bovell decided he could wait no longer for starting the flight. At this time, the wind was blowing fresh from the north-west and increasing, and there were heavy rain squalls, with much low cloud. The visibility was, however, good near the surface, except during rain squalls.

There were still some hours of daylight, as sunset was not till fifty minutes past midnight.[2] The scene from the *Victorious'* spray-swept flight deck was an uninviting one of breaking seas and driving rain clouds. The nine aircraft were divided into three sub-flights. The first was led by Lieut.-Commander

---

[1] It is now known that the *Bismarck's* behaviour did not originate in a desire to catch the *Suffolk* napping but was intended to cover the breaking-away of the *Prinz Eugen*, who was now to make her separate way to an oiler.

[2] This statement needs perhaps a word or two of explanation. In the first place, the ships were keeping double British summer time, which meant that their clocks showed 10 p.m. when it was really 8 p.m. at Greenwich. But they had also now reached a point a long way to the west of Greenwich, the longitude of the *Victorious* at this time being about 35 west. This was more than two hours behind Greenwich by the sun. The ships' clocks were therefore more than four hours ahead of the sun; which meant that if the ships' time of sunset was 12.52 a.m., the real time of it was 8.52 p.m.

92

Esmonde; the second by Lieutenant P. D. Gick, R.N.; and the third by Lieutenant (A) H. C. P. Pollard, R.N. Two Fulmars went with them. As he saw them all safely get off, Captain Bovell reflected that it would be a good deal harder to get them back.

A little more than an hour later, at about 11.30 p.m., the aircraft, with the help of their A.S.V., spotted what they thought was the *Bismarck* through a break in the cloud about twenty miles distant and went back into cloud to close. When they came out again they could not see her but found themselves close to the British shadowing vessels. The *Norfolk* noticed that the aircraft were streaking off in the wrong direction in the misty weather. She made frantic signals to the leading aircraft to tell it the bearing of the enemy, which it eventually took in. Thereafter each sub-flight asked the *Norfolk* for guidance as it passed over her on its way to the attacking course.

At this critical juncture, a totally unexpected complication arose to influence the attack. Shortly after being directed on to the right course for the enemy by the *Norfolk*, the aircraft picked up an object on the radar which they naturally assumed to be the *Bismarck*. At the right instant, they broke cloud cover in a good attacking position; only to find to their astonishment and disappointment that the target object was not after all the *Bismarck* but a strange vessel,[1] which fortune had chosen this of all moments to place in this particular spot on the ocean. The *Bismarck*, it is true, was also in sight and not far off. But the false attack against the stranger had given the Germans valuable time to get their anti-aircraft weapons into action, and as the Swordfish approached they were met by a heavy volume of flak.

The attack was pressed home with great gallantry. All nine machines dropped their torpedoes. One of the pilots, Lieutenant Gick, had been an Instructor at the torpedo school. Unperturbed by the heavy anti-aircraft fire from the *Bismarck*, he went out again and came in to drop his torpedo in a better position. As the machines roared away after making their attack they

[1] She was the American Coastguard cutter *Modoc*—Lieutenant-Commander H. G. Belford, U.S.C.G.

were able to see at least one torpedo take effect. Shortly afterwards, those on board the *Victorious*, who had endured a seemingly interminable wait since the aircraft had taken off, were overjoyed to receive a signal that the attack had been carried out and that one hit was claimed.

Soon after the *Victorious'* aircraft had disappeared in the direction of the *Bismarck*, a considerable stir was caused on the *Norfolk's* bridge by the sudden end-on appearance in the mist of a vessel just before the starboard beam, which to the Flag-Captain and several others had the distinct outlines of a battleship. The Flag-Captain was sure he could see turrets and ordered a quick turn away to port. The Rear-Admiral was not so sure. He could see, he said, a yellow mast and did not believe it belonged to the *Bismarck*.[1] However, as the *Norfolk* circled round he, knowing nothing about any American or other vessel in the vicinity, concluded that it must have been the *Bismarck* after all, and he hoisted the signal for the *Prince of Wales* to open fire. As it happened, the latter's answering pendant jammed, and the Rear-Admiral was in some agitation that an opportunity of firing at the *Bismarck* was being lost. Meanwhile the ship, whatever it was, had disappeared. But a signal came in from the *Prince of Wales* that she was not convinced it had been the *Bismarck*.

The aircraft were now on their way back to the *Victorious*, and Captain Bovell was full of apprehension about their safe return. The majority of the pilots had not landed on a ship's deck before they had flown on to the *Victorious* four days before. The two or three practice landings they had been able to do before leaving for this operation had all been in daylight. Never had they landed on a carrier at night. It was now rapidly becoming dark—darker than Captain Bovell had anticipated. The night before, there had been twilight all night. But that had been almost on the latitude of the Faroes, and Captain Bovell had not realized how much to the southwards he had come in the previous twenty hours. He was, in fact, now level with Aberdeen; and it made a good deal of difference.

---

[1] The *Modoc* had a yellow mast and upper works.

94

To make matters worse, the *Victorious'* homing beacon was discovered to have gone out of action, and so the returning aircraft could not be guided back to the carrier by this means. In his anxiety, Captain Bovell waited till the aircraft should have been nearing the ship and then switched on all his searchlights and flashed them round the heavens. He was promptly ordered by the Vice-Admiral of the escorting cruisers, fearful of attracting enemy submarines, to switch them off. Captain Bovell, who was much more concerned to get his aircraft back, delayed switching off until the receipt of a second signal, when he felt obliged to obey. But he then started a long signal to the Vice-Admiral with a very bright signalling searchlight, asking permission to switch on again. Before this signal was completed, however, he heard the welcome sound of aircraft in the distance.

By now it was pitch dark, raining heavily, and there was considerable motion on the ship. As he turned into the wind for the landing on, Captain Bovell frankly had little hope that any of the aircraft would get on to the deck in safety. There was, however, not a single crash, every aircraft landing on in some sort of fashion. Lieutenant Commander Esmonde came up to the bridge to report. He thanked the Captain for the searchlights, but said that the first lights the aircraft had actually seen were the red signalling lamps of the cruisers.[1]

The Commander-in-Chief had received the aircraft's wireless report of their attack and of having scored one hit with much satisfaction; for he knew how heavily inexperience and bad weather had weighted the scales against the airmen. He thought, as he remarked to his Chief of Staff, that they had done very well to have got off the *Victorious* and found the enemy at all, let alone to have scored a hit.

But what was of chief importance to him was what that hit had done and whether, especially, it had reduced the enemy's speed. This latter would probably not become known immediately, till the shadowing cruisers had had time to notice a reduction of speed and also to be sure that it was not a tem-

---

[1] Ironically enough, these lamps had been specially designed to reduce the distance at which they would be visible.

porary one. As midnight passed and one o'clock without any such report coming through, Sir John Tovey came ruefully to conclude that the urgently desired slowing-up of the enemy had not been effected. Still, the underwater damage resulting from a torpedo hit would increase the likelihood of an early return to a dockyard.

It had been a pretty miserable day in every way. Beginning with the painful and utterly unlooked-for setback of the defeat of Vice-Admiral Holland's squadron, there had followed the so far fruitless chase of an enemy who might still manage to avoid being caught. It did not make matters any pleasanter that the Commander-in-Chief's destroyers were now leaving him for harbour. The long high-speed dash had depleted their tanks too much for them to remain with him longer, and by midnight they had all parted company en route for Iceland. Their disappearance left the Admiral with a nasty naked feeling, especially since he knew from the shadowing ships' reports that the *Bismarck* was now zigzagging, which might well mean that U-boats were known by her to be in the vicinity and that she was wanting to insure against mistakes of identity.

The Admiral was also aware that the *Repulse* could only stay a few more hours. She had just about enough fuel left to fight the action early next morning that Sir John hoped to bring off. But should there be any delay, she would have to part company about 9 a.m. Altogether, it was a somewhat grim reversal of fortune since the corresponding time the day before, when the *Bismarck's* career seemed as good as over. There was, however, even worse to come.

Not long after the air attack, there was a short interchange of shots between the *Prince of Wales* and the enemy. From one or other of the German ships in the gathering darkness ahead there came the flashes of gunfire, but the fall of shot was not seen.[1] The *Prince of Wales* replied with two salvoes, but ceased fire owing to the difficulty of spotting the fall of shot in the failing light.

[1] Presumably, it was not the *Prinz Eugen*, since she had broken away some hours before.

96

8. H.M.S. *Prince of Wales* as seen from H.M.S. *Norfolk* just after the action of May 24th

9. The *Norfolk's* bridge on May 24th showing, left to right, the Officer of the Watch, Rear-Admiral Wake-Walker, Captain Phillips, and the Midshipman of the Watch

10. Sir James Somerville

May 25th

Shadowing dispositions for the night were then taken up. The *Prince of Wales* was placed astern of Norfolk and the Rear-Admiral signalled to the *Suffolk* that she was to act independently for the operation of her radar. The other two ships would conform to her movements. Some hours before, he had congratulated her on her very fine shadowing and had told her they might have to rely on her again during the night. As a result of the redisposing of the force, she was now well up towards the *Bismarck's* port beam and about ten miles away from her. All the British ships were zigzagging against submarine attack, a warning that the British forces might be running into U-boat concentrations having been sent out by the Admiralty some hours before. The bearing of the enemy being what it was, the *Suffolk's* zigzag kept on jeopardizing her contact with the enemy. On the outward leg, the *Suffolk* not only opened the range from the *Bismarck* but her radar came near the after limit of its effective arc and sometimes got shut off. But on the inward leg, contact would be picked up again. So Captain Ellis went on for about two hours, occasionally losing radar touch as he zigzagged out, and finding it once more on the leg back.

Had the *Suffolk* been occupying her previous position fairly fine on the enemy's quarter, the zigzag would have had no such risky element. Moreover, the placing of all three shadowing ships on one side of the enemy was of itself distinctly hazardous, since it left his starboard side entirely unguarded. If the *Bismarck* had radar, as she might have, she would presumably soon become aware that there was no British ship to starboard of her and that a way of escape in that direction was open.

Presently, radar touch was again lost by the *Suffolk* on her outward zigzag. But this time it was not regained on the inward. Captain Ellis went on with the inward leg, hoping and expecting to pick up contact again at any moment. The minutes passed, however, without the welcome mark re-appearing on the screen. In his report, Captain Ellis considers he was slow in realizing that touch had actually been lost. If he was, it was not surprising. His brain was numb with cold and fatigue. He had had no sleep for four nights. For the past thirty hours, he had been under the continuous heavy strain of unflagging watchfulness, punctuated by alarms, ambushes, and shellfire, while he was frozen to the bone through the breaking of the bridge screens hours before.

When he did fully grasp that the *Bismarck* had given him the slip, Captain Ellis made a quick appreciation of the situation. It seemed to him that the enemy must have either turned right round to starboard and have passed under the sterns of the shadowing vessels, or have made some alteration to the westward and at the same time put on her utmost speed—she had previously been doing only about 16 knots for some time—in order to get clear ahead. In Captain Ellis's view at that moment, the increase of speed was the most dangerous possibility. If the enemy had done this, he might well gain an unchallengeable lead unless quick action was taken to follow him at high speed. Captain Ellis felt that, as so far the only person in the know, he must take this action himself and he therefore rang down for full speed. Thus when he came to make his report that the enemy had got away, he was able to include a brief estimate of what the enemy might have done and to say what action he himself was taking. By now, an hour had passed since the last enemy report and the time was 4 a.m.

The *Suffolk's* signal announcing the loss of contact was taken in by both the *King George V* and the Admiralty. Sir John Tovey, was snatching some sleep when the signal came through. But the news that the enemy had at last shaken off pursuit brought him back to the plotting-room.

In naval operations, the question of the fatigue of the senior officers presents only too often a most difficult problem. If contact or near contact with the enemy is prolonged, as it is liable to be for days on end, Admirals and Captains are more than likely to be faced sooner or later with this dilemma. Things happen so fast at sea that at any moment the situation may take a crucial turn which calls for an instantaneous decision on the highest level. Are the Admirals and Captains therefore to remain on their bridges or at least awake and in continuous touch with events until they fail through exhaustion: or are they to try to get a reasonable amount of sleep and risk not becoming acquainted with vital information, either through not being there to see things themselves or through not being told of important occurrences by subordinates anxious to shield them from avoidable disturbance? Their whole upbringing and training will undoubtedly induce them to keep awake. Captain Ellis, though remaining up himself, sent his navigating officer down for an hour or two's sleep during the chase. Similarly, Captain Phillips, when darkness closed down on this night, cleared his non-watch-keeping officers off the bridge and sent them to rest while he stayed looking out.[1]

The correct solution is unquestionably that Admirals should delegate responsibility to their Chiefs of Staff and Captains to their seconds-in-command so that they themselves can obtain sufficient rest to 'keep going'. But one can nevertheless sympathize with the senior naval men who try to retain control too long. Air Marshals have little need to give their supervision to bombing raids after the aircraft have taken off. An Army Commander is usually some miles from the fighting-lines, and on land the decisive moment which requires his personal attention usually gives some warning of its approach. At sea, however, the crisis on which everything hangs may develop in a flash, and senior naval officers would be less than human if they did not wish to be there to deal with it. Actually, Rear-Admiral Wake-Walker did decide that he and his Flag-Captain should split the night between them. In consequence, the Rear-Admiral was asleep when contact was lost and for about an hour afterwards. It would have been much more difficult for Captain Ellis, who at this time was bearing the immediate responsibility for maintaining contact, to get any rest.

Artificial aids can, of course, be used. About one o'clock on this particular night, the Surgeon Commander of the *Norfolk*, aware that the Rear-Admiral and Flag-Captain had been without sleep for forty hours or so, appeared on the bridge and

---

[1] This problem of fatigue is particularly acute in the case of aircraft carriers whose captains, in addition to ordinary tactical preoccupations, have all the flying on and off to tax their strength.

offered them some benzedrine tablets. They both took some; but later, when the effects had worn off, paid the inevitable price of feeling worse than if they had not done so.

CHAPTER 6

Where is the Bismarck?

The enemy ships had escaped from their shadowers who had held on to them with great skill and persistence under very unfavourable circumstances for thirty-one and a half hours. How had they done so, where were they now, and in which direction were they going? These were the questions that faced Sir John Tovey and his operational staff officers when they gathered in the *King George V's* plotting-room in the darkness of the early morning.

The *Bismarck's* likely intentions had been exhaustively debated the day before, when the Admiral had decided that there were three main possibilities:

(1) She might be making for a rendezvous with an oiler, most probably either in the Davis Strait area or somewhere well south near the Azores or Canaries.

(2) She might be making for a dockyard on the Atlantic coast or in the Mediterranean.

(3) She might be returning to Germany for repairs.

It had been decided then that none of these possibilities could be ruled out and that each must receive consideration. The same would hold good next morning unless anything had happened in the meanwhile to affect the argument. There was only one thing that might have done so: the claim of a torpedo hit on the *Bismarck* by the *Victorious'* aircraft. It was not certain that this hit had occurred, but it was probable. If it had, a ship so modern and well-built as the *Bismarck* could undoubtedly carry one torpedo hit without undue embarrassment, unless it were in

101

Where is the Bismarck?

a very awkward place, which there was no reason to think had been the case. The *Bismarck* had been steaming quite fast—over 20 knots—for a time after the air attack, and she could hardly have done so had she received really serious damage. The torpedoes used against her were aircraft torpedoes, then only 18-in. ones, as compared to the 21-in. destroyer and submarine torpedoes against which modern battleships were designed to be protected.[1]

The one torpedo hit—if it had happened—would certainly increase the chance of the *Bismarck* being bound for a dockyard for repairs, but hardly to the complete exclusion of her prior engagement in raider operations. It was, in fact, advisable to regard all the previous day's possibilities as still valid.

That being so, searches for the missing enemy were required in at least four directions: north-west for Greenland; between south and south-west for a course towards the Azores-Canaries region; between south-east and east-south-east for a retreat to Brest, St. Nazaire, Ferrol, Gibraltar or Dakar; and between about north-east and north-north-east for a return to Germany. It was, however, clear to Sir John Tovey that he had not the means for making all these searches simultaneously, and that he would therefore have to decide on some order of search priority. Thus confronted, he fell back once more on the principle of choosing the enemy course of action most dangerous from the British point of view; which as before, he judged to be an escape to an oiler rendezvous somewhere between south, through west, to north-west. These directions should, therefore, be the first to be investigated. If the *Bismarck* were bound directly for a dockyard, she would be doing no harm to allied shipping for the time being. Hence, the primary concern was to ensure against her being bent on operations against shipping at this moment.

A beginning had, indeed, already been made of these searches by the shadowing cruisers on their own initiative. After losing contact, Captain Ellis of the *Suffolk* guessed that the *Bismarck* had sheered off to the westward with a view to putting on a lot

---

[1] Admiral Lutjens reported by signal that this torpedo hit was 'of no importance'.

102

more speed and then turning back to gain a decisive lead on her previous southerly course. After a westward cast, therefore, he signalled that he was resuming the course of the enemy as last known. A little later, when Rear-Admiral Wake-Walker had had time to take in the situation, he thought it more likely that the enemy had gone off on a permanent westerly or south-westerly course. Accordingly he signalled to the *Suffolk* to cover that possibility, in obedience to which Captain Ellis made a large alteration to starboard to a course of about south-west. After another half-hour (at 6.30 a.m.) the Rear-Admiral signalled that his flagship *Norfolk* would search in a direction 285 degrees, or a little north of west. He added, however, that he thought the enemy might have 'cut away' under the cruisers' sterns. The fact that, while envisaging that the *Bismarck* might have gone east, he had decided to act on the supposition that she had gone almost west gave indirect support to the Commander-in-Chief's opinion that an early return to a dockyard by the enemy could not be regarded as a foregone conclusion.

The Rear-Admiral also reported to the Commander-in-Chief about this time that he was sending the *Prince of Wales* to join Sir John's flag. This was a reasonable step to take. The *Prince of Wales* had been kept with the cruisers while there was a chance that they might need her armoured support. Now that they had lost the *Bismarck*, the question of support against her was no longer an immediate issue, and there was a good deal to be said for sending the *Prince of Wales*, as a battleship, to swell the Commander-in-Chief's battle force, especially as the latter had closed in considerably on the shadowing ships and was now not far off.

Sir John Tovey could thus conclude that enemy courses from about south-south-west to about west-north-west were being covered by the *Suffolk*, *Norfolk*, and *Prince of Wales*. He himself continued on as he was for an hour or two and then took his squadron round to about west-south-west, to augment the westerly coverage. The obvious ships for dealing with the Greenland sector between west-north-west and north were the 2nd Cruiser Squadron and *Victorious*. The latter with her attendant cruisers had presumably fallen far astern while flying aircraft off and on again the night before, during which processes she would have had to steam head to wind, or nearly at right angles to the *King George V's* course. The Commander-in-Chief therefore told Rear-Admiral Curteis to cover the north-westerly sector by means of an air search by *Victorious'* aircraft, to start from the *Bismarck's* last reported position. They were actually close to that position at this time and so the *Victorious* could begin the air search without delay.[1]

By this time, the *Repulse* was too short of fuel to remain longer with the fleet. The Admiralty, knowing this, had just signalled that she should go to Newfoundland for oil; and her passage thither would afford some measure of search in a west-south-westerly direction.

Such was the situation as it was seen by Sir John Tovey on board the *King George V.* How was it being viewed by other units not in company with him? The *Rodney's* Captain had been pressing on south-west all night at his best speed to get across the enemy's line of advance. After what had happened to the *Hood's* squadron, he did not feel at all happy about the adequacy of the *King George V–Repulse* combination to deal with the *Bismarck,*[2] and he wanted to get the *Rodney* on to the scene as soon as possible. He had the destroyers *Somali, Mashona* and *Tartar* with him most of the night, but the weather got steadily worse and the destroyers could not keep up with the *Rodney* without fear of damaging themselves in the mounting seas. Captain Dalrymple-Hamilton felt that three good destroyers would be very useful to the Commander-in-Chief could they be produced. But he thought it more important that the *Rodney*

[1] As a matter of fact, Captain Bovell had concluded almost as soon as he heard of the loss of contact, that the *Bismarck* was making for Brest; and he had signalled over by lamp to Rear-Admiral Curteis for permission to fly off a search at daylight along the course (south-east) for that port. Before this could be begun, however, there came the Commander-in-Chief's order for the air search to be made to the north-west; and so the south-easterly search had to be cancelled.

[2] Sir John Tovey was also dubious about the *Repulse's* ability to stand punishment from the *Bismarck*. On the 24th, when an action early on the 25th was expected, he had told her to keep 5,000 yards outside the *King George V* and not to engage before the latter had opened fire.

should get into position quickly, if necessary by herself, than that she should arrive more slowly with her destroyers in company with her. Just after half-past three, therefore, he slipped the destroyers and took the *Rodney* on alone.

When he learnt, an hour and a half to two hours later, that the *Bismarck* had been lost at about 3 a.m., he was practically south-east of the position where she had last been seen. He and his Operations Committee set to work to appreciate the situation, just as Sir John Tovey was doing at that very time in his flagship to the north-westward. To the *Rodney's* Captain and Committee, the likely courses of action for the *Bismarck* appeared to be two. She might be going back to the North Sea, either north or south of Iceland. Or she might be making for a French or Spanish port. There was, in their view, much to be said for a Spanish port.[1] The Spanish Government was apparently in open sympathy with the Axis Powers and was indeed under a considerable obligation to them for their help in the Spanish Civil War. If the *Bismarck* therefore put into a Spanish port—which would probably be Ferrol—for repairs, she could presumably be assured of a friendly reception, while the refits to British warships then in progress in American yards would provide the Spaniards with a ready-made precedent for putting her to rights without interning her. Moreover, the British, being still all alone against the Axis, would not be wanting any more countries to join their enemies, and the *Bismarck* might well count on being repaired in Ferrol without disturbance by bombing, which she would certainly undergo in Brest or St. Nazaire.[2] There was also the parallel of the *Goeben* and *Breslau* of the previous war to keep in mind, in which fugitive German ships had made for neutral Turkish territory and had thereby succeeded in bringing Turkey into the war on the side of Germany.

Of the two alternatives, the North Sea or an Atlantic port,

---

[1] Extract from German Naval archives: 'There could be no doubt about the gravity of the *Bismarck's* situation at that time (25th May). . . . In view of this situation, the Naval Staff suggested to the Fleet Commander to consider putting in at a harbour in northern Spain, should further developments make such action necessary.'

[2] St. Nazaire was the only French Atlantic port where she could be docked.

the *Rodney's* Committee were inclined to favour the latter. Assessing the possible torpedo hit on the *Bismarck* and her oily wake in much the same way as the Commander-in-Chief and his staff, the Committee considered that such injuries as the *Bismarck* may have received were probably moderate enough to be repaired in an Atlantic yard, and that there was therefore no imperative need for the ship to return to Germany. She was likely also to be imagining that the British were busy organizing stiff opposition to her re-entry into the North Sea. The chance of making an Atlantic port would probably appear to her more promising.

Thus argued the *Rodney's* Committee, with Captain Dalrymple-Hamilton 'in the chair'. It did not occur to its members to consider an enemy move to the north-west or the south-west, about which Sir John Tovey was mainly anxious. But then the *Rodney* could have done next to nothing to counter an enemy escape in those directions.

Having decided for an Atlantic port, Captain Dalrymple-Hamilton turned once again to the chart. For dealing with an enemy course to a French or Spanish port, the *Rodney* was excellently placed. At 6 a.m., she had been almost on the direct line between the *Bismarck's* last reported position and Ferrol. She was about 100 miles beyond (i.e. to the south-westward) of the direct line to Brest. The *Bismarck* might not, of course, be going direct to either of these ports but might be making a detour out in the Atlantic before turning east for her destination. The course she had been steering before being lost indicated such a detour; and this course, if prolonged, would pass about 100 miles beyond (to the south-west of) the *Rodney's* present position. The *Rodney* was, in fact, in a very happy situation: she was on one of the enemy's three most likely lines of advance and was midway between the two others. She was, moreover, very comfortably —about 350 miles—in front of the *Bismarck* if the latter were steering any of these three courses, and therefore had plenty of time to move over to one side or the other should further news of her movements come through. The most sensible thing, therefore, seemed to be for the *Rodney* to stay more or less where she was for the time being, to see how the situation developed: and this was what Captain Dalrymple-Hamilton decided to do. It would also have the advantage of allowing the *Rodney's* destroyers, ploughing along behind in bad weather, to catch her up.

The *Ramillies* at this time was 400 miles south of the *Bismarck's* last reported position. In Captain Read's view, the *Bismarck* was probably making for a secret rendezvous in the southern part of the north Atlantic, to reach which he estimated that she would pass a little to the westward of him. He therefore steered north-west to get to the westward of her, according to his last instructions.

The *Edinburgh* was rather more than 300 miles south-east of the *Ramillies*, and was at this time steering direct for the point where contact with the *Bismarck* had been lost. Knowing that the *Ramillies* was to the westward of him, Commodore Blackman thought he could best go on as he was, thus covering an enemy course of about south-south-east, or more or less for the Straits of Gibraltar.

The *London* had already been directed to look for the German tanker near the Canary Islands and was not recalled.

Vice-Admiral Somerville with Force H was a long way— about 1,300 miles—to the southward. He was obviously too far off to have any immediate influence on the situation and could only continue his north-north-westerly course. Just before midnight and while the *Bismarck* was still under observation, he had been told by the Admiralty to steer to intercept her from the southward; and these instructions were still governing his actions. His problem was therefore an easier one than that facing a number of other officers. But his personal opinion at this time was that the *Bismarck* was very likely to be making for Brest, with Ferrol as a close alternative; the latter for reasons similar to those which were causing the Captain of the *Rodney* to consider that port.

The general sweep to the westward by the Home Fleet ships began about 6.30 a.m. and went on for nearly five hours.[1]

[1] See Diagram 4.

Where is the Bismarck?

At 8 a.m., the *Rodney's* destroyers overtook and rejoined her. At 9 a.m., the *Repulse* was detached to fuel and she went off towards Newfoundland by herself. Knowing from intercepted signals that the *Repulse* was going, Captain Dalrymple-Hamilton felt that the time was ripe to tell the Commander-in-Chief where the *Rodney* was and what she was doing. The Admiral had so far heard nothing from the *Rodney* and might well be in some doubt of her whereabouts and intentions. At 9 a.m., therefore, Captain Dalrymple-Hamilton made a signal giving his position and saying that he proposed to remain in that vicinity to intercept an enemy break to the south-eastward; that he had the *Somali, Mashona* and *Tartar* in company; and that the visibility was ten miles. This was the only wireless signal he made throughout the operation.[1]

In the middle of the forenoon, when the ground intended to be covered by the westward searches had nearly been swept out, a most important signal from the Admiralty was received by the Commander-in-Chief. Shortly after the *Victorious'* torpedo-aircraft attack of the night before, one of the two German ships, presumably the *Bismarck*, had made a long wireless signal. A few hours later, the *Bismarck* had succeeded in shaking off pursuit and disappearing into the blue. Then, a few hours later still, when she was well and truly lost and all the British authorities were racking their brains to know where she could be, the same ship that had transmitted by wireless the night before began a series of transmissions again; or, at least, it seemed to be the same ship.

If it were the *Bismarck*, as there was at least some cause for thinking, her use of wireless at this time seemed a wantonly risky proceeding. For if enemy wireless direction-finding stations could pick up her wireless waves and obtain bearings of their point of origin, some estimate of the ship's position might be made. This could quite well undo most of the value of her escape from the shadowing cruisers by telling the British authorities

---

[1] Captain Dalrymple-Hamilton had been reluctant to break wireless silence before; since, being so favourably placed for intercepting *Bismarck*, he did not want to give his presence away.

where she now was.[1] Wireless bearings were, in fact, being obtained from the signals in question, and these bearings were the core of the very important signal that Sir John Tovey received from the Admiralty shortly after 10.30 a.m. The signal told him that recent directional interceptions gave bearings of the enemy transmitting, thought to be the *Bismarck*, of so many degrees from a particular directional station, and so many degrees from various others at 0852 (8.52 a.m.). These bearings were not ideal in that they were all from stations in the United Kingdom. This meant that, since the enemy ship concerned was far out in the Atlantic, the bearings from the different stations were almost parallel. Had there been a greater geographical variation between the receiving stations—had, for instance, Gibraltar also been able to make a contribution—there might have been a wide enough angle between the outer bearings to have given a reliable 'cut', providing an exact position. But Gibraltar was too far away to help in this respect; and, as it was, the bearings indicated little more than a latitude.

However, it was possible to deduce quite a lot from even this. The Admiralty signal had merely given the bearings and their associated stations and had included no estimate of the enemy's position as plotted (as it presumably had been) in the Admiralty.[2] But the bearings could also be plotted in the flagship, and no time was lost in doing so. The 'latitude lines' when drawn on the *King George V's* chart varied. One or two were to the south of the enemy's last reported position. But the bulk of them were to the north of it. Accepting the majority bearings to the northward of the *Bismarck's* last position as being the most reliable, it was finally estimated in the *King George V* that the *Bismarck's* probable position at 8.52 a.m. had been 57° N., 33° W., the natural deduction from which was that she was on the way back to the North Sea. This position the Commander-in-Chief broadcast to the Home Fleet at 10.47 a.m. and directed ships to search

[1] We now know that it *was* the *Bismarck* who was signalling; but not from any reckless incaution. It was just that she did not believe in her own good fortune in throwing off her pursuers, but imagined that they were still following her by radar, though she could not see them.

[2] It is difficult to understand why this was omitted.

accordingly. He did not tell them where to search but left it to them to draw their own conclusions from the enemy position he had given.

Hardly any of them seems to have been in doubt as to what was implied. The *Suffolk*, about to report all enemy courses from south to nearly south-west for enemy speeds of up to 22 knots covered and clear, suppressed this report and turned towards Iceland. The *Prince of Wales*, who had converged quite a lot on the *King George V* but had not actually sighted her, turned round and steered for the Denmark Strait. The 2nd Cruiser Squadron and *Victorious* made for the Iceland–Faroes gap, carrying out air searches as they went. The *Ramillies*, who had been steering north-west in the belief that the *Bismarck* might be coming south-south-west, also complied with the Commander-in-Chief's signal, but without much enthusiasm. If the *Bismarck* were really making for the North Sea, the *Ramillies*, old, slow and, on this assumption, 400 miles behind her, was clearly out of the running. Indeed, an hour or two later there came a signal from the Admiralty for her to find the *Britannic* and escort her to Halifax. Sir John Tovey's own flagship had, of course, been the first to turn towards the North Sea.

Only two of the ships under Sir John's orders took a different line. The *Rodney* did not comply with the Commander-in-Chief's signal, because Captain Dalrymple-Hamilton felt it could not be meant to apply to him. He was hundreds of miles away from the *Bismarck*, and if she were making for the North Sea there would be no conceivable hope of the *Rodney* intercepting her. On the other hand, the *Rodney* was so admirably placed for countering a move to the south-eastward that it seemed better to leave her where she was on the bare chance that the *Bismarck* might after all be going that way. Captain Dalrymple-Hamilton therefore continued 'marking time'; and, an hour later, as if in corroboration of his judgment, he received a signal from the Admiralty directing him to act on the assumption that the enemy was making for a Bay of Biscay port. This presumably meant either Brest or St. Nazaire, the two most likely repair ports for the *Bismarck*; but the enemy's course would be near enough the same to either of them. The *Bismarck* might not, of course, be going direct to her real destination. But Captain Dalrymple-Hamilton felt that if the Admiralty had not meant him to cover the direct course, it would have said so. He was, as already mentioned, about 100 miles to the south-westward of the direct line to Brest, and the quickest course to reach that line was therefore north-east. He consequently turned in that direction. He was now steering the same general course as the bulk of the Home Fleet, though for a different reason.

The other ship that took a separate line was the *Norfolk*. By the time Sir John Tovey had received and plotted the directional bearings of the enemy ship, Rear-Admiral Wake-Walker had already come to the conclusion that the enemy was making for Brest, and he decided, in spite of the Commander-in-Chief's signal, to move in that direction. One reason he had for doing so was that, while there were plenty of cruisers steaming towards the Iceland passages and several others already in them, there was only one cruiser, the *Sheffield* (with Force H), moving to cover Brest; and the Rear-Admiral thought the *Norfolk* could usefully make a second. Even so, her course (100 degrees) was not very whole-heartedly in that direction, the ship pointing for Ireland instead of for the Brest Peninsula, suggesting that the Rear-Admiral was perhaps a little conscious of his unorthodoxy.

Of the ships not under the Commander-in-Chief's orders, Force H had been steering, in accordance with Admiralty orders received during the night, to intercept the *Bismarck* from the southward.[1] A few minutes before Sir John Tovey's 10.47 signal went out for the search north-eastward, Sir James Somerville had received a new Admiralty instruction to assume the enemy to be making for Brest. That being so, Sir James felt himself unaffected by Sir John Tovey's signal indicating an enemy course towards the North Sea.

There was also the *Edinburgh*. She, it will be recalled, had been a long way south-south-east of the *Bismarck's* last reported

[1] The question of whose orders Force H was acting under is referred to again in a later footnote. Up to this point, however, there can be little doubt that it was operating directly under the Admiralty, which had just been giving it specific orders. Much the same applies to the *Edinburgh*.

position and had been steering straight for it. When most of the Home Fleet turned towards the Iceland passages, she, like the *Ramillies*, was too far south to be of much use in a north-easterly chase. Commodore Blackman, therefore, decided to work on the Brest hypothesis, and he began a curve of search based on that assumption.[1] Thus, apart from Force H, all ships were making back for the North Sea except the *Rodney*, the *Edinburgh* and the *Norfolk*, which were looking towards Brest, the *Norfolk* albeit with something of a squint.

Meanwhile, on shore in England, various people had also been appreciating the situation. First and foremost among these were, of course, the officers of the Naval Staff at the Admiralty. To them, from the First Sea Lord downwards, the position, course, and speed of the *Bismarck* formed the burning question of the hour.[2] Among the senior members, opinion in the early stages seems to have been somewhat fluid. At all events, about 10 a.m. Captain C. S. Daniel, the Director of Plans, and Captain R. A. B. Edwards, the Director of Operations, were sent for and told to make separate appreciations and report their conclusions. Each officer was to work entirely independently of the other.

After about an hour's investigation and thought, Captain Daniel returned to the War Room and gave it as his considered opinion that the *Bismarck* was making for a French port. His reasons were that the *Bismarck* was damaged, apparently not seriously but certainly enough to necessitate some repairs. Hence she was probably on the way to a dockyard, which meant either in Germany or France. To reach Germany she would have to pass the (to her) enemy line Scotland to the Denmark Strait, a line which she would naturally suppose was in rapid process of being made as dangerous as possible for her by means of aircraft, sub-marines, destroyers, cruisers and perhaps a battleship or two. On the other hand, if she made for a French port, she would reach friendly air cover without having to run the gauntlet of enemy shore-based air attack. She would, of course, have to take her

---

[1] A curve of search is a scientific way of conducting a search for an enemy, based on assumed limits of course and speed.

[2] Though the First Sea Lord and the V.C.N.S. had also to keep in close touch with the Cretan situation, in which the Mediterranean Fleet was heavily involved

chance with the ships that had been and were doubtless still chasing her. But she was in the open Atlantic, and would probably think there was more chance of evading or repelling them than of successfully passing through the dangerous area north of Scotland en route to Germany.

Those to whom Captain Daniel made his report included the First Lord, the First Sea Lord, the Vice-Chief of the Naval Staff, and one or two other high officers. His impression six years afterwards[1] was that this opinion of his was none too welcome. He could not say that any one particular member of his audience was or was not hostile to his conclusions. But his recollection was that there was a certain criticism in the atmosphere, even though it may have been expressed by only one of those present. Such criticism was, so far as he remembered, based on the argument that because there was in fact very little naval force left to guard the Scotland–Denmark Strait line and because the weather was still very adverse to air operations, the *Bismarck* was likely to be making for this virtually unguarded way home.

Whether Captain Edwards reported before or after Captain Daniel is uncertain, but it was probably at much about the same time. His appreciation was very similar to his colleague's. He, too, thought the *Bismarck* would be making for a French port. His recollection of the reception of this view differs, however, from that of Captain Daniel concerning the latter's almost identical conclusion. Captain Edwards has told the author he feels reasonably sure that his opinion fell on sympathetic ears.

This latter impression receives the general support of the then Third Sea Lord, now Admiral Lord Fraser. Though not at the time a member of the Naval Staff, he was keeping in close touch with the progress of the operation owing to his responsibility for the repair of any damaged ships. In a letter to the author on this subject, he said that: 'I had many talks with the V.C.N.S. and A.C.N.S. (H), and I am quite sure the opinion was held that she [the *Bismarck*] would go to France but that some safeguarding of the Iceland–Faroes gap was desirable.' This statement of Lord Fraser's makes it quite clear that a French port was the

---

[1] As communicated verbally to the author.

favourite choice of at least two high members of the Naval Staff. What remains, however, a little in doubt is whether this had been their choice from the first news of the *Bismarck* being lost or whether their opinion had changed at all since before Lord Fraser's talks with them began.

As to the possible movement of opinion in the Naval Staff, it is to be noted that at 7.30 a.m. the Director of Operations at the Admiralty (Captain Edwards), in telling the naval liaison officer at the headquarters of Coastal Command of the loss of contact, said that the Admiralty wanted air preparations made in case of an enemy break-back through the Denmark Strait. At 11.50 a.m., Captain C. Meynell, R.N., the senior naval liaison officer at Coastal Command Headquarters, who had just gone up to the Admiralty, telephoned back to his headquarters that the latest Admiralty appreciation was that the *Bismarck* had steered due east at about 23 knots from the time she was lost until 10 a.m. and had then turned to a course of 120 degrees (about south-east by east, or direct for Brest). Anyone who believed that the *Bismarck* had been steering due east during the seven hours between 3 a.m. and 10 a.m. could hardly fail to connect such a course by her with the possibility of a return to the North Sea. If, therefore, this report of Captain Meynell's was correct,[1] it may well be that up till 10 a.m.—and perhaps later—at least someone in high authority at the Admiralty was attaching considerable weight to a return by the enemy to Germany. But it is also possible that the opinion expressed to Captain Meynell that the *Bismarck* had turned towards Brest at 10 a.m. was that of the officers of the Operations Division (we have already seen that the Director of Operations held this view) and was not necessarily shared by the members of the Board.

At Coastal Command Headquarters they had also been appreciating the situation. As soon as he heard of the *Bismarck's* escape, Air Marshal Sir Frederick Bowhill, the Commander-in-Chief, sent for Captain Meynell and another naval officer on his staff, Commander D. V. Peyton-Ward, R.N., and together they settled down to consider where the *Bismarck* was going

[1] It was recorded in writing at the time at Coastal Command Headquarters.

and what action Coastal Command should take to find her. Sir Frederick was well qualified to preside at such a conference. Having been a merchant service and also a naval officer before becoming an airman, he was able to conduct an essentially nautical appreciation with an expert knowledge of sea conditions and a full appreciation of the naval point of view.

On the first point, he and his two naval assistants reached much the same conclusion that Captains Daniel and Edwards were simultaneously arriving at in Whitehall. The *Bismarck* was going either back to Germany or on to France for repairs; and, of the two destinations, the French was the more likely. Did Coastal Command possess enough long-range aircraft at this moment, it would certainly be desirable to cover both possibilities. But it was woefully short of them; and consequently it was best to devote the limited resources available to the most likely enemy course of action—the continuance on to France. Sir Frederick Bowhill thought the *Bismarck* was making either for Brest or St. Nazaire (almost the same course) but that she would first steer down into the southern part of the Bay of Biscay and finally turn north-east or north towards the selected port. As an old seaman himself, he felt convinced that the *Bismarck*, after a long detour out into the Atlantic, would not think of making a landfall at the Brest Peninsula itself. It was a vile coast, rockbound and tide-ridden and now devoid of navigational aids. Any sensible navigator would make his first landfall at Finisterre where the coast, though rocky, was less dangerous, and where C. Finisterre light was still burning.

These conclusions reached, Sir Frederick told the Command Navigator, Wing-Commander Crofton, to work out suitable searches on the basis decided, and despatched Captain Meynell to the Admiralty (about an hour's journey) to explain to the Naval Staff what was proposed and why. Wing-Commander Crofton's searches, after approval by Sir Frederick Bowhill, would be telephoned up to meet Captain Meynell on his arrival at Whitehall.

They consisted of a parallel-track search by three Catalinas from 58° N. on a track of 240° to 28° 40′ W., then 180° for forty miles, and then 118° to datum line 028° from 50° N., 20° W. After presenting this search plan to the Naval Staff, Captain Meynell found that the Admiralty would like the searches flown in the reverse direction, the first leg to be shortened by 120 miles, the last leg to be extended by 180 miles, and the patrol to be extended to 29° W. Two Catalinas left at 1.50 p.m. and the third a quarter of an hour later on these amended sweeps.

To return now to the fleet. It will be recalled that Sir John Tovey had interpreted the directional bearings received at about 10.30 a.m. as meaning that the *Bismarck* was returning to the North Sea, and had ordered his fleet to search accordingly. Most of the ships had turned towards Iceland and had continued to steam back in that direction. Just about an hour after they had begun to do so, Sir John intercepted the Admiralty's signal to the *Rodney* telling her to assume the *Bismarck* was making for a Bay of Biscay port. This was hardly compatible with the Home Fleet's return towards the North Sea, of which the Admiralty should by then have been well aware, but it could be explained on the supposition that the Admiralty thought the *Rodney* too far south to be of use in a north-easterly chase.

Two more hours passed without incident. At half-past two, Admiral Tovey intercepted another signal from the Admiralty to the *Rodney*, this time instructing her to cancel her Bay of Biscay orders and conform to Sir John Tovey's signal of 10.47 a.m. which had started the Home Fleet steering north-east.[1] This set at rest any misgivings Sir John may have felt at the *Rodney's* earlier instructions to assume a Bay of Biscay destination for the enemy. The Admiral's sense of added assurance was, however, to be short-lived.

At half-past three, he received a fresh estimate of the enemy's position from the Admiralty, based on wireless directional bearings obtained at 1.20 p.m. (1320). This time, the bearings were not signalled by the Admiralty for the Commander-in-Chief to plot. The enemy position as plotted in the Admiralty

---

[1] This change of orders actually made no difference to the *Rodney*. She had been steering roughly north-east to get across the line to Brest. The same course, if prolonged, would do equally well for the North Sea. Captain Dalrymple-Hamilton, not for the first time during the operation, just went on as before.

was passed out, and was given as being within a fifty-mile radius of 55° 15′ N., 32° W. The implication of this position—which was stated by the Admiralty to be a fairly reliable one—was unmistakable. It could only be that the *Bismarck* was making, not for the North Sea, but for the Bay of Biscay.[1]

The receipt of this information in the *King George V* gave rise to some hard thinking there. Could the flagship's estimate of the enemy's position at 8.52 a.m. possibly have been wrong? The officer who had plotted the bearings asked himself if by any chance he might have made a mistake. There was a way of checking the accuracy of the plotted bearings by calculation; and he began to work them out. The calculations gave different results to the plot. Instead of showing the majority of the bearings lines as being to the north of the *Bismarck's* last position, as the plot had done, the greater part of them now came to the south of it. The message of the 0852 bearings needed therefore to be changed. They did not, after all, point to a return to the North Sea but to a continued progress towards a French port. Moreover, the 0852 and the 1320 bearings were both in agreement on this matter. Hence, if there were any value in these directional bearings at all, it must follow that for nearly five hours the fleet had been steaming on a false trail.[2]

This agitating discovery was immediately brought to Sir John Tovey's notice. But Sir John, while appreciating the momentous import of the corrected enemy position for 0852, found this and the new one for 1320 difficult to reconcile with other happenings. If his own signalled position for the enemy at 0852 had been wrong, why had not the Admiralty told him so? They must have plotted the 0852 bearings in the Admiralty, and presumably have obtained a different result from his. His own, as it now appeared inaccurate, enemy position had been in the Admiralty's possession for a good four and a half hours; yet they had said not a word about its possible falsity, even though he might be hurrying in the wrong direction in consequence thereof. It

---

[1] See Diagram 4.

[2] The cause of the original plot having been inaccurate is highly technical, but can briefly be described as being due to insufficient graduations on the chart supplied for plotting.

was very strange. The Admiralty could surely not be letting him make a mistake of this gravity without pointing it out to him.

There were also the two Admiralty signals to the *Rodney* which, from being reasonably consistent with the previous situation as Sir John Tovey had known it, had now become wholly incomprehensible. If both the 0852 and 1320 wireless bearings indicated an enemy course towards the Brest Peninsula, what on earth could have induced the Admiralty, an hour after the second set of bearings had confirmed the first, to tell the *Rodney* to turn back for the North Sea?

Sir John Tovey did not know what to make of it all. On the evidence now at his disposal, he felt that his proper course was to turn round and steer for Brest. Yet he hesitated to do so. He had been steering towards the North Sea for a number of hours. Not only had the Admiralty not objected, but they had just told the *Rodney* to do it, too. Sir John felt that some inquiry was called for before he made so drastic a change of strategy. At about half-past four, therefore, he asked the Admiralty if they thought the enemy was making for the Faroes? There was a long wait for a reply without any being received. After an hour and a half, Sir John could bear the silence no longer. At ten minutes past six he altered his flagship's course for Brest and told the Admiralty he had done so. But before his signal had reached Whitehall, the Admiralty had reached the same decision. A signal had been drafted telling the *Rodney* to go back to the original assumption that the *Bismarck* was making for a French port. Then, twenty minutes later, the Admiralty set all doubts at rest by dropping all question of the North Sea. A signal was sent out that the Admiralty considered that the *Bismarck* was making for the west coast of France. This signal was received in the *King George V* at about a quarter past seven. Admiral Tovey had gained an hour by backing his own judgment.

So they had been engaged on a wild-goose chase after all. For approximately seven hours the main portion of the British hunting forces had been pressing back to the north-east on the assumption that the enemy was retreating towards the North Sea, when all the time he had really been pushing on for the west coast of France.

On receipt of the Admiralty's appreciation, the *Suffolk* concluded she was now out of the chase and went on steering for Iceland. The 2nd Cruiser Squadron and *Victorious* also continued in that direction. The cruisers were too short of fuel to go any farther towards Brest, and Vice-Admiral Curteis considered that *Victorious* could not be sent on unescorted. So he took her with him. The *Prince of Wales*, damaged and short of oil, had already been told to return home. Thus, though the Commander-in-Chief had turned towards Brest, seven of his ships—one battleship, one carrier, and five cruisers—did not turn after him but stood on for the North Sea.

The *Norfolk* also went on in that direction for some time. It will be remembered that instead of initially returning towards the North Sea with the bulk of the fleet, the Rear-Admiral had steered towards the south of Ireland. He continued in this direction until 6 p.m., when he came across the *Prince of Wales* steering for the North Sea. Deciding that lack of fuel prevented him going on any further towards Ireland, the Rear-Admiral turned to imitate the *Prince of Wales*. But when the Admiralty's final choice of the Bay of Biscay as the *Bismarck's* true destination was made known, the Rear-Admiral's urge to remain in the hunt began to reassert itself. After an hour and a half's conflict between his fighting instincts and his fear of running out of oil, he decided to throw caution to the winds and turned back to join the rest of the pack.

The Commander-in-Chief now had time to go into how much ground had been lost by the unfortunate run to the north-eastward; and the estimates he received in that connection filled him with gloom. At three o'clock in the morning, when the *Bismarck* had just been lost, he had been well abreast of her and was expecting to be able to engage her by 9 a.m. on the 25th. The present position was far less favourable. It was soon obvious, even from rough calculations, that the long deviation towards the North Sea had cost the British ships many miles of headway. From having been practically level with the enemy, they must be now a good 100 miles behind him.

Where is the Bismarck?

Was there any chance of being able to make good those 100 miles? If the enemy were doing only 22 knots (he might be doing more), and Sir John Tovey's flagship went flat out at say 29 knots, it would take fourteen hours to recover the lost ground. But of such very hard steaming for so long a period the *King George V* was no longer capable. The curve of fuel expenditure begins to mount very steeply as full speed is approached. The flagship had already had almost three days' steaming, for the last day and a half of which she had been rushing along at high speed after the *Bismarck*; and the fuel situation was now so bad that protracted bouts of nearly full speed could no longer be contemplated. Sir John Tovey could not now safely average more than about 25 knots and perhaps not that.

The fuel position was, indeed, causing him the gravest concern. He had known before he left harbour that fuel might prove troublesome if the operation were to be long drawn out, and for that reason had remained in harbour till the last practicable moment. His apprehensions in this respect were now being realized. The destroyers with the *Hood's* squadron had been left behind after the action on the morning of the 24th, and Sir John's own destroyers had been forced to turn back that night. The *Repulse* had dropped out at 9 a.m. of this day (the 25th), and the Admiral's cruiser screen and aircraft carrier had now departed, too. The one remaining ship of his original force, the *King George V*, was also getting unpleasantly short. The day before, Sir John had had his attention drawn to her declining reserves of fuel by his Flag-Captain, who would naturally be in the closest touch with the ship's fuel state. With his customary cheerfulness, Captain Patterson had tried to gild an unwelcome subject with a little humour. 'I am in the position, sir,' he said to the Admiral as he handed him the statement of the flagship's percentages of fuel expended and remaining, 'of your Bank Manager, whose duty it is to see that you do not acquire an overdraft,' though Sir John actually needed no warning as to the dwindling condition of his account.

Altogether, the *Bismarck's* unwitting indiscretion in giving a clue to her position by making wireless signals had had the most unlooked-for results. So far from bringing the hunting ships swarming in on her from numerous points of the compass, it had had exactly the opposite effect of sending them streaming off in the wrong direction.

What was it that induced the Admiralty to acquiesce for so long in the Commander-in-Chief's false cast? We know from Lord Fraser that the Vice-Chief of the Naval Staff and the Assistant Chief (Home) both believed in the French destination of the *Bismarck*, anyway for most of the day. So did the Directors of Operations and Plans, certainly from 11 a.m. onwards. In the Coastal Command diary for May 25th, there is an entry, timed 2 p.m., recording the receipt of the news of the 1320 enemy position by direction-finding (D /F). Under this entry is a note which says: 'In the light of the most recent D /F bearings of the enemy, it appears that he is making a more southerly course than previously appreciated,' an opinion which, in view of the close and almost continuous consultation between Coastal Command and the Admiralty at this time, can probably be taken as reflecting the views of the Naval Staff.

Indeed, by 2 p.m., the evidence in favour of a French port was getting very strong. The searches to the south-west, west, and north-west had produced no sign of the enemy. The searches to the north-east, which had then been in progress for three hours, had been equally sterile. The one uninvestigated sector was the south-eastern, and it was in that sector that both the 0852 and the 1320 D /F bearings indicated the enemy to be. How was it that in spite of these highly suggestive pointers towards the south-east the fleet continued, with the full knowledge of the Naval Staff of the Admiralty, to steer north-east for another four to five hours? The author does not know. But in view of all the evidence in support of a French port and of the widespread opinion known to be prevailing among members of the Naval Staff that that was where the *Bismarck* was going, he feels it to be a fair inference that there must have been some powerful influence at work, for a reason that is so far obscure, to keep the fleet steaming towards the North Sea for so long.

As a result of the 1320 D /F bearings, another change was

made in the current Catalina sweep. The aircraft were already in the air but could be reached by wireless. They were now told to search on, and seventy miles each side of, a line drawn 298° from a position 52° N., 22° W., as far as the longitude of 30° W., thence 360° for fifty miles, thence 060° to longitude 16° W.[1]

The aircraft received these new orders and proceeded accordingly. Most of the area was covered during darkness. The centre aircraft exchanged signals with the *Edinburgh* at about midnight, and the right-hand aircraft at about the same time saw what she thought was one battleship and four destroyers, which, however, did not reply to the challenge. An hour later, the centre aircraft passed over the wake of an unknown ship, which also did not reply to signals.[2] The Catalinas landed between 10.30 a.m. and noon on the 26th, after nearly twenty-four hours in the air.

Meanwhile, during the evening of the 25th, Sir Frederick Bowhill, with his two naval liaison officers and Wing-Commander Crofton as before, was considering what searches to arrange for the next day. They were not, of course, doing it in isolation. There was frequent telephonic consultation between one of the naval liaison officers and the Director of Operations at the Admiralty and occasionally between one of the Chiefs of the Naval Staff and Sir Frederick Bowhill himself. It was a cordial process of mutual help. Sometimes Coastal Command plans would be altered to accord with what the Admiralty wanted. Sometimes Admiralty requirements would be adjusted to meet Coastal Command capabilities or views.

By means of this joint machinery, it was decided to have two crossover patrols to be operative by 9.30 a.m., one patrol to be to the southward of the other. The northernmost patrol would cover the enemy courses from the direct line to Brest to the middle of the Bay. The southernmost patrol would cover courses from the middle of the Bay to Cape Finisterre. This latter patrol was arranged at the instigation of Sir Frederick himself. So strong was his seamanlike feeling that the *Bismarck* would make her landfall on the south side of the Bay that he would not

---

[1] See Diagram 5.
[2] This may have been the *King George V.*

be denied a search covering that line; and to this the Admiralty eventually agreed, provided the more northerly search was flown as well.

During the day, arrangements were being made by the Admiral (Submarines), Sir Max Horton, to establish a line of submarines across the approaches to Brest. Six submarines were ordered to take up positions approximately 120 miles from that port. In the evening, orders were sent out to them to move the line southeast to cover St. Nazaire.

CHAPTER 7

The Bismarck Re-discovered

N ight fell on the 25th of May over a turbulent sea. It was blowing hard from the north-west and the glass was still dropping. For Sir John Tovey the day had been no improvement on its predecessor. The false scent that he and the bulk of his forces had evidently been following for so many hours had brought about a most lamentable deterioration in the situation. Much priceless ground had been lost, ground that had been won by so much hard steaming on the two previous days. There was reason to fear that the enemy battleship was now not only ahead of the *King George V*, but a long way ahead.

It was no use disguising the fact that the *King George V's* chances of overtaking the *Bismarck* were now distinctly questionable. Of the other northern British forces—those that had started from the United Kingdom and Iceland—still in the hunt, it appeared from intercepted signals that the *Norfolk* was about 100 miles north-north-west of the Commander-in-Chief, and therefore even farther away from the *Bismarck*. The *Rodney* should be somewhere ahead of the *King George V* and thus better placed, but of her position Sir John had no reliable information. She and the *Ramillies* had been put under his orders by an Admiralty signal earlier in the day. But in the afternoon the Admiralty had intervened again and ordered *Ramillies* to take over escort of the *Britannic*; so she was no longer available. The *Rodney* had made no signal since the early part of the forenoon, when she had said she was remaining where she was. She had since received several signals of instructions from the Admiralty, as Sir John knew, each one cancelling the last. The *Edinburgh* had made no signal at all since contact with the *Bismarck* was lost. Admiral Tovey, while confident that she and all other separate units had been steering the best courses to intercept according to the information available, could nevertheless make only rough estimates of their present positions.

The frequent situation reports passed out by the Admiralty during the previous day had come to an end early that morning (25th), the last one having been issued at 6 a.m.; further reports being presumably prevented by the disappearance of the enemy and by the growing uncertainty regarding the positions of the British forces. Indeed, the *Rodney's* signal giving her 9 a.m. position showed up the danger of the Admiralty's authority being attached to estimates of ships' positions which were based on pure guesswork; for that signal revealed the Admiralty's assumed position for the *Rodney* to be no less than 220 miles in error. At the time of her one signal, the *Rodney* had reported having three destroyers in company. They might or might not be still with her; and if they were, Sir John could not tell how much longer they would be able to remain.

There was, of course, Force H to the southward. This force had not been placed under Sir John's orders, but could nevertheless be regarded as coming within the orbit of his personal control.[1] The two forces, Sir John Tovey's and Sir James Somer-

[1] As a matter of fact, the command relationship between Force H and the Commander-in-Chief is an interesting question. Sir John Tovey evidently regarded the Force as being under his orders at some period of the operation, for in his dispatch he says that 'the disposition of Force H, *Rodney* and the other forces placed at my disposal'. . . . An inquiry by the author of the Admiralty, however, drew the reply that 'no definite order was issued placing Force H at the Commander-in-Chief, Home Fleet's, disposal'. Sir James Somerville has told the author that he has no record in his Report of Proceedings of being placed under the orders of the Commander-in-Chief, Home Fleet. But he points out that the fact of his own dispatch being addressed to the Commander-in-Chief implies subordination for the purposes of the operation.

In normal naval procedure, the senior officer on the spot takes automatic command, and the Admiralty's letter to the author went on to say that 'there is little doubt that the Commander-in-Chief felt at perfect liberty to give orders to Force H or to any other force or ship in the area of operations'. The questionable point, however, is the definition of an 'area of operations'. Could Force H be regarded as within the area of operations for the purposes of command when it was 1,000 miles or more away from the Commander-in-Chief and was in receipt of direct orders from the Admiralty? It is difficult to think so. But if not, at what point does a distant but approaching force come within the 'operational area'?

ville's, had been steadily approaching each other for some days, and in about twenty-four hours' time should be in operational contact. Twenty-four hours or so earlier, before the *Bismarck* had been lost and while Sir John Tovey still hoped to sight her about 9 a.m. on the 25th, Force H had been 1,500 miles or so to the southward, and seemed to him to be too far away to play a part in the operation. But as he now, after dark on the 25th, surveyed the general position, he realized that, as matters stood, this Force might well be the only remaining obstacle to the *Bismarck's* arrival in harbour. He had never supposed that the *Renown* and *Sheffield* could stop her by gunfire. The only real hope lay in the *Ark Royal's* aircraft. If they could get in some attacks, they might be able to slow the *Bismarck* up. It had to be remembered, however, that these attacks, if they eventuated, would represent only the second occasion in history of a battle-ship at sea being attacked by carrier aircraft: the first being the very recent one of the *Victorious'* aircraft attack on the *Bismarck* on the evening of May 24th, which had not been an over-whelming success. True, the *Victorious'* air crews had been almost entirely raw and untrained, while the *Ark Royal's* crews were at that time the most experienced and efficient carrier air-men in the Navy. But even the latter had been hampered by war conditions in carrying out the best form of training—dummy attacks with real torpedoes[1] set to run under the target ship. Such attacks necessitated the recovery of the torpedoes and con-sequently had to be done in waters free of enemy submarines, the opportunities for which were inevitably rare. Moreover, so great was the then general shortage of naval aircraft that the *Ark Royal* seldom carried more than two-thirds of the full com-plement of aircraft that she could accommodate. In estimating, therefore, her chances of effecting a decisive reduction in the *Bismarck's* speed, it was prudent for optimism to be restrained, especially in view of the foul weather prevailing.

Sir John Tovey was also acutely aware that all British ships were running into more and more danger. If the *Bismarck* was really making for a French port, as the Admiralty thought (and

[1] Fitted, of course, with 'practice' non-explosive heads.

126

he thought, too) it was only to be expected that the German shore authorities would arrange concentrations of submarines to cover her approach, probably supplemented by air attacks from airfields in occupied France and night attacks by German destroyers believed to be based on Brest and other French bases. For these reasons, the fact that he had no escorting destroyers left with him was a cause of no small concern to the Commander-in-Chief, since it would mean that the *King George V* and also possibly the *Rodney* would be left unprotected against submarine attack and unduly vulnerable to the other forms of enemy hostility. About 10.30 p.m., therefore, he sent a signal to the Admiralty asking if a destroyer screen could be made available for both ships.

At the Admiralty, it happened that Captain Edwards, Director of Operations, was already working on this very question. It had been known in the Admiralty since the early morning, when the first of them arrived in Iceland, that the Commander-in-Chief's destroyers had left him, and there had been anxious consultations at intervals during the day among the senior members of the Naval Staff as to how some more could be provided for him. It was a question easier asked than answered. The battleships were a long way—about 800 miles—from land, and any spare destroyers leaving harbour in the United Kingdom to meet them would, if they were to effect a junction in time to be of use, have to know fairly exactly where to make for; and this, for most of the day, was what no one could tell, the doubts about the *Bismarck's* direction of escape leaving the future movements of the chasing ships very much in the air.

Moreover, to add to the difficulty, there were no spare destroyers. Far from it. At this stage of the war there was an acute shortage of them; and those which were not refitting, repairing, or boiler-cleaning were being hustled off to sea with another convoy almost as soon as they had brought one into harbour. For these reasons, the problem of getting some more destroyers out to the Commander-in-Chief had seemed an insoluble one.

However, in the early part of the night, as Captain Edwards, with the Commander-in-Chief's need for anti-submarine protection ever in mind, was studying the plot with one or two of his 'Operations' staff, he suddenly realized that an opportunity for meeting this need had at last presented itself. It had only become clear in the last hour or two that the *King George* and *Rodney* were now finally committed to a course for the Bay of Biscay. On this course, the battleships were rapidly closing Convoy WS8B which, with an anti-submarine escort of five destroyers, was about 300 miles fine on their starboard bow. If the convoy's destroyers could be transferred to the Commander-in-Chief, they should be able to join him by the early afternoon of the next day. Here was the chance to give the big ships the anti-submarine protection they so sorely required.

The convoy and its escort being under the orders of the Commander-in-Chief, Western Approaches, Admiral Sir Percy Noble, Captain Edwards proceeded to ring up Commodore Mansfield, Sir Percy's Chief of Staff, to raise with him the question of the destroyers' diversion. He and the Commodore discussed the situation. The convoy had got well to the westward, and according to available intelligence there were no U-boats in that part of the ocean through which it was about to pass. To remove the convoy's destroyers was not therefore an acutely risky proceeding, though naturally neither the Admiralty nor Western Approaches would wish to do it from choice. But if either the convoy or Sir John Tovey's battleships had to go bare of escort, it would be better for the convoy to feel the cold. On this there was agreement on both sides: and so it was decided. But five destroyers were not enough for two battleships who were probably not in company. Three at least were needed for each. So Western Approaches, after a careful overhaul of its resources, said that one more, H.M.S. *Jupiter*, could be produced as well; though as she was still in the Irish Sea she could not join up till well after the others. As all six destroyers were under the immediate command of Sir Percy Noble, it was finally arranged that he should send out the necessary orders to them to make for the Commander-in-Chief.

While this consultation as to ways and means of keeping Sir

John Tovey supplied with destroyers was in progress, the signal from Sir John came in asking for it to be done: and later in the night, when the Prime Minister looked in to see how the chase was going and expressed concern over Sir John Tovey's lack of destroyers, the First Sea Lord was able to tell him that reinforcement had been arranged.

The five destroyers with the convoy all belonged to the 4th Destroyer Flotilla, commanded by Captain Philip Vian, who was present in H.M.S. *Cossack*. This was the Captain Vian whose name was already known to his countrymen as the rescuer of the *Altmark's* prisoners in a Norwegian fiord early in 1940. Besides his own *Cossack*, he now had with him the *Maori*, *Zulu*, *Sikh*, and the Polish destroyer *Piorun*. Conscious of the important nature of his convoy, it had not occurred to Captain Vian to leave it on his own responsibility. He was, however, aware of the general situation from intercepted signals and had been passing on a running commentary to Vice-Admiral Geoffrey Arbuthnot, the Commander-in-Chief designate in the East Indies, who was proceeding to his station in one of the ships of the convoy, the *Georgic*.[1]

It was two o'clock in the morning of the 26th before the signal went out to Captain Vian to take *Cossack*, *Sikh* and *Zulu* to join *King George V* and to send *Maori* and *Piorun* to *Rodney*. Captain Vian gathered his escort together and, saying good-bye to the convoy, joyfully made off to the north-eastward.

[1] Concerned to avoid creating alarm in Sir Geoffrey Arbuthnot's ship by indicating in plain language that the *Bismarck* and *Prinz Eugen* were at sea and coming down towards the convoy, Captain Vian used a rough-and-ready code which he hoped would convey the news to Sir Geoffrey and no one else. Some of the signals, for the use of which the author is indebted to Admiral Arbuthnot, follow:

'Wake found the Beaver and another thought to be Marlborough's friend in Hamlet Sound last evening and still hangs on. Kerr steps in this morning and quickly took the count whilst Leach arriving later took and believed gave a punch. Beaver and friend followed by Wake moving south-west fast.'

1325/24th.

'Beaver at 1800 59·43 N. 36·15 W. 180. 24 with Wake following. Jack and Freddie will be in picture to-morrow morning if he holds on and we shall be later still if he decides to join Salmon and Gluckstein.'

1800/24th.

'Add to my 1800. James left to meet us unless otherwise diverted.'

1827/24th.

The Bismarck Re-discovered

Meanwhile, Sir James Somerville to the southward was also weighing up the situation and making his plans for the next day. His last instructions, which he had received at about 11 a.m. on the 25th, were to act on the assumption that the *Bismarck* was making for Brest. An hour or two later, he became aware that the whole of Sir John Tovey's force, with Admiralty acquiescence, was streaking back north-eastward on the supposition that the enemy was returning to Germany. As Force H's assignment to cover Brest had not been altered, Sir James concluded that it was because he was too far off to do anything in the North Sea direction, and so might just as well be left to carry on with his original orders. However, by eight o'clock in the evening it had become clear that a French port was now the generally favoured destination and that the whole hunt, or such as were left in the field, had turned and were hurrying down towards the Bay of Biscay.

Sir James Somerville had two main preoccupations. The first and principal was the rediscovery of the *Bismarck*. Assessing the enemy's maximum speed since last seen at 25 knots, the Vice-Admiral's idea was to make a series of air searches during the 26th for enemy speeds of from 25 knots down to 15 knots. He discussed the technical aspects of the problem with Captain Maund of the *Ark Royal* during the daylight hours of the 25th, their respective views being flashed backwards and forwards by signalling searchlight across the mile or two of water that separated their two ships. Eventually, it was decided to carry out three searches. The first, to start shortly after daylight, would be for enemy speeds of from 25 to 21 knots. If that failed to locate the enemy, the next search, which should begin about 1 p.m., would be for speeds of 21 down to 18 knots; and if a blank were still drawn, there would be a third search in the evening for 18 to 15 knots.

The first search area was to be that enclosed by the positions 47°, 30′ N., 21°, 30′ W.; 49° 00′ N., 23° 40′ W.; 52° 25′ N., 20° 00′ W.; and 51° 40′ N., 17° 00′ W. This area extended across and somewhat beyond what were thought to be the most likely enemy courses and was deep enough to cover the higher enemy speeds mentioned above. The search was to commence at 7 a.m. on the 26th.

It was not, however, only the problem of finding the *Bismarck* that was exercising Sir James Somerville's mind. He had for more than a day been worried about the *Scharnhorst* and *Gneisenau*. These two battle cruisers had reached Brest several months before, and when last seen by British aircraft on May 23rd were still there. But this report was now two days old, and the two German heavy ships might well have come out in the interval if they meant to meet and accompany the *Bismarck* back to harbour. And what more natural than that they should do this, if they were able to? Their fleet mate was damaged and was almost certainly being chased by a number of British men-of-war, who might be able to intercept and bring her to battle. If the *Scharnhorst* and *Gneisenau* could join forces with her, the combined German squadron would possibly be strong enough to fight off any British gun attacks. There had, it is true, been claims of damage inflicted on the two ships in Brest by the air attacks frequently being made on them by Bomber Command. But reliable confirmation of such damage was difficult to obtain, failing which it was advisable to assume that they were ready for sea.[1]

Sir James Somerville had hoped by this time to have had more information about them. He had detached his destroyers at 9 a.m. that morning to return to Gibraltar for fuel. Before they went, he ordered their senior officer to make two signals when he was 150 miles clear; one informing the Admiralty of the position, course, and speed of Force H at 7.30 a.m., and the other to the Commander-in-Chief, Plymouth, asking for full information about the results of the aerial reconnaissance of Brest. Nothing, however, had as yet come through from Plymouth, not even negative information that the weather was preventing such reconnaissance being carried out. This lack of news was irritating, for Sir James wished to employ all his available aircraft for the search for and attack on the *Bismarck*, but was

[1] Captured German records in fact show that the two battle cruisers were under repair from bomb injury at this time and could not have gone out.

anxious about doing so without some reassurance about the German battle cruisers.

He had intended to carry out his own air search for them during the 25th. But the weather had been very unfavourable. The clouds were low and dense rain squalls kept on being encountered. Twice during the day the aircraft on anti-submarine patrol were recalled on account of poor visibility; and the extended security search for the *Scharnhorst* and *Gneisenau* had had to be cancelled. The Vice-Admiral accordingly told the *Ark Royal* that the first anti-submarine patrol aircraft which went out in the morning were to have a look round for the two ships.

As the night progressed, the wind gradually increased. The ships of Force H, on a course of north, had the sea nearly ahead. They were punching more and more heavily into it and began to ship very big seas. There was danger of smashing the ships up, and it became imperative to reduce speed to prevent damage. It was brought down first to 23 knots, then to 19, and finally, about one o'clock in the morning, to 17 knots.

Twilight grew into daylight over a gale-swept sea, the circle of ocean white with breaking waves. The *Renown*, in spite of her reduced speed, was throwing up fountains of spray as she drove into the sea, her bows periodically scooping up solid masses of water which washed surging up against her foremost turrets. The *Ark Royal's* flying deck, much higher up, was being constantly soused with spray, and every now and then the ship would even bury her nose so deep as to take a green sea over this deck, sixty-three feet above the normal water-line. Captain Maund sent two specialist officers down independently to measure the rise and fall of the stern by sextant, and they returned to report fifty-three and fifty-six feet respectively. The operation of naval aircraft had not previously been attempted under such conditions.

Nearly 300 miles to the north-westward, the *King George V* was corkscrewing along at 24 knots with the wind and sea behind her. Of the fifteen ships that had been in company with the Commander-in-Chief on the morning of May 23rd, she, his flagship, was the only one left, all the others having departed to refuel. Fine on her port bow but still well below the horizon were the *Rodney* and the destroyers *Somali*, *Mashona*, and *Tartar*, steering a slightly converging course, their position still unknown to Sir John Tovey who, steaming at higher speed, was gradually overtaking them. Also on the port bow, her presence as yet quite unsuspected, was the *Edinburgh*, last reported by the Admiralty as 350 miles south-west of the *King George V's* present position, steering north-west. Commodore Blackman's movements had, in fact, taken him across into close proximity with the *King George V* and *Rodney*, both of whom he was to sight during the forenoon. His curve of search having been completed during the night, at 1.30 a.m. he had altered course towards the Bay of Biscay.

In the *Ark Royal*, notwithstanding the high seas and the heavy motion on the ship, the dawn patrol had got away shortly after 7 a.m. The next item on the flying agenda was the first of the main searches for the *Bismarck*. The successive reductions of speed forced upon the squadron during the night had put the *Ark Royal* two hours behind programme time. She could not now reach the commencing point for the first reconnaissance flight until about 9 a.m., instead of 7 a.m. as planned. As all delay was to the prejudice of the later searches, Captain Maund obtained the Vice-Admiral's signalled approval for moving the search area thirty-five miles to the south-eastward, by which means the take-off could be made before 9 o'clock. At 8.30 a.m. the ten Swordfish for the reconnaissance were brought up from below. Ranging so many aircraft on the wet, slippery and heaving flying-deck was a very tricky business. Even with extra men for holding the aircraft down, several slipped bodily across the deck in the heavy rolling of the ship and were only just saved from going overboard.

At 8.35 a.m., the ship turned into the wind and reduced speed to 10 knots for the fly-off. The first aircraft to go gathered way, faltered as the ship rose to a wave, increased speed again as the bows began to fall, and was clear. The others followed quickly in a jerky procession which kept Captain Maund's heart in his mouth as he gazed down from the bridge. In the *Renown*, the

The Bismarck Re-discovered

Vice-Admiral and other officers had their binoculars glued to the *Ark Royal's* flight-deck in parallel anxiety about the take-off. All the aircraft, however, got off safely and the three-and-a-half-hour search had begun. In the hangars, six more Swordfish with long-range tanks were being got ready to go up for shadowing duty the moment the enemy was found. The *Ark Royal* herself turned north across the eastern side of the search area, this being the direction the aircraft had been told she would steam while they were up, the landing-on position to be fifty miles north of where the Swordfish had taken off.

For two hours there was silence. Then, suddenly, British wireless operators began to write down a signal. It was an aircraft report of a battleship in a position 49° 33′ N., 21° 50′ W., steering 150 degrees (approximately S.E. by E.).[1]

Was it the *Bismarck*? In dozens of plotting-rooms, the position was being quickly measured off on the chart. The pencilled point with its small enclosing circle was well away from any British heavy ship. In the *King George V*, they made it 135 miles almost due south; in the *Rodney*, 125 miles south by west; in the *Renown*, 112 miles west-north-west. Though none of these ships knew exactly where the other two were, each knew that neither of them was likely to be in the reported direction. The *Ramillies*, too, would be several hundreds of miles from the signalled position. It was, therefore, probable that the strange battleship actually was the *Bismarck*. The joyful news was broadcast to ships' companies and brought delighted smiles to the faces of officers and men. The loss of contact with the *Bismarck* and the long period during which she had remained undiscovered had weighed on everyone's spirits. Now, thank goodness, she had been found again. She had been shadowed for thirty-one and a half hours by *Norfolk* and *Suffolk* before she managed to give them the slip. It had taken exactly thirty-one and a half hours to resight her.

It was not, however, the *Ark Royal's* Swordfish that had made the welcome discovery. Five hours before these had switchbacked

---

[1] It was followed a few minutes later by an amplifying signal saying the battleship's speed was 20 knots.

their way off the *Ark Royal's* seesawing deck, two Catalina air-craft of Coastal Command had taken off from Lough Erne in Northern Ireland to carry out the crossover searches which had been decided on the evening before. It had been 3 a.m. when they left, and as they flew on for hour after hour out into the Atlantic, night had faded and daylight had spread over the ocean, and the crews were able to observe a heavy sea running below them. At 10.30 a.m., one of the Catalinas (Z of 209 Squadron) sighted a ship. The scene has been graphically described in *Coastal Command*, the Air Ministry handbook:

' "George" (the automatic pilot) was flying the aircraft', said the pilot, 'at 500 feet when we saw a warship. I was in the second pilot's seat when the occupant of the seat beside me, an Ameri-can, said: "What the devil's that?" I stared and saw a dull black shape through the mist which curled above a very rough sea. "Looks like a battleship," he said. I said: "Better get closer. Go round its stern." I thought it might be the *Bismarck*, because I could see no destroyers round the ship and I should have seen them had she been a British warship. I left my seat, went to the wireless operator's table, grabbed a piece of paper and began to write out a signal.'[1]

This was the signal that first told the British forces and shore authorities that the *Bismarck* had been found again. Her position as given by the aircraft, when joined to her position as last reported by the *Suffolk*, showed that during the hours she had been lost she had not been steering direct for Brest or St. Nazaire but almost straight for Cape Finisterre. This was what Sir Frederick Bowhill had been expecting her to do, and had consequently been so insistent that one of the two crossover searches should cover this possibility. It was the aircraft assigned to this duty that had sighted the enemy.[2]

---

[1] It is interesting that the pilot should have taken the lack of destroyers as the main evidence of enemy character. The *King George V* at this time also had no destroyers with her, and had Z/209 sighted her first he would presumably have reported her as an enemy. Owing to his own error in position, Z/209 would have reported this 'enemy' as being thirty-five miles astern of the *King George V*; and it is an intriguing speculation what action the Admiral and the Captain of the *Rodney* would have taken on such a report.

[2] See Diagram 5.

The Bismarck Re-discovered

Z /209 had taken cloud cover on first sighting the strange battleship. Nine minutes later, she inadvertently broke cover right above the ship, which opened fire on her. No one was hit but the hull was holed in a number of places. In taking avoiding action, the aircraft lost touch with the hostile vessel and did not find her again.

This loss of contact was fortunately only a temporary embarrassment. The *Ark Royal's* broad-fronted air search was coming up from the south-east and would soon be combing the area where the enemy ship had been seen. Half an hour after the Catalina lost touch, one of the Swordfish sighted the same enemy ship. She reported her as a cruiser. By the standing orders, the next aircraft on the sweep should move in to make contact as well; and, sure enough, ten minutes later there came another Swordfish report, this time of a battleship.

The cruiser classification of the enemy ship by the first Swordfish inevitably damped some of the pleasure felt by the higher officers at her discovery, by raising doubts whether she was the *Bismarck* or the *Prinz Eugen*. The two ships had much the same silhouette and deck plan and exactly the same arrangement of turrets and guns. It would not be difficult to make a false identification: and doubts on this score, once engendered, could not properly be dispelled until there had been a chance to interrogate the pilots and observers. As soon as the Catalina's original report came through, Vice-Admiral Somerville had instructed the *Ark Royal* to fly off two shadowers with long-range tanks to join her and also to obtain a check on her position which, after many hours' flying, might be some way out.[1] Until these new shadowing aircraft arrived on the scene, the first Swordfish shadowers (now the only ones in touch) could not return for questioning. It was two hours before they landed on and the crews went up to the bridge for interrogation. Under examination, they could not be certain whether it was the *Bismarck* or the *Prinz Eugen* they had seen. At first they said they thought it was the *Bismarck*; but when pressed admitted it might have been the smaller ship. It was hard, they said, to be sure; and, indeed, one can sympathize

[1] It was thirty-five miles in error.

136

with them. Vice-Admiral Holland, with his much greater experience, had mistaken the *Prinz Eugen* for the *Bismarck* two
days before.

Knowing these first shadowers were back, Vice-Admiral
Somerville in the *Renown* was pressing for news of their verbal
reports. Captain Maund had to reply that there was only one
enemy ship and that the evidence favoured her being the *Prinz
Eugen*. He added, however, that he himself was sure she was the
Bismarck. How could he tell? The evidence, as he admitted, was
the other way. Yet, without having seen for himself, he was prepared to go against the evidence.

Captain Maund had formulated several arguments in support
of his signalled opinion. But, in truth, what really counted with
him was the feeling in his bones that this was the *Bismarck* and
none other. A somewhat unscientific and perhaps incautious
basis for a strategical judgment. Yet he was right. It was indeed
the *Bismarck*, as eventually became clear beyond doubt as the
reports of the later shadowers came through.

CHAPTER 8

Aircraft Attack the Wrong Ship

====

Captain Vian was steering with his five destroyers to meet the *King George V* and *Rodney* when he received the Catalina's report of a battleship. It put the enemy ship some way to the south-eastward of him. He was then about three hours' steaming from a junction with the British battleships. Concluding at once that it was the *Bismarck* that had been seen, Captain Vian asked himself the questions, should he go on to rendezvous with the *King George V* and *Rodney* or should he make for the enemy? It took him very little time to decide for the enemy. It was true that he had definite orders to join the Commander-in-Chief. But he considered this was one of those occasions when an officer should be ready to ignore his instructions. It was obvious that the enemy had a substantial lead on the British battleships, and therefore equally plain that there was urgent need for slowing him up. Perhaps his, Captain Vian's, destroyers might be able to help in that. Of course, if he did not join up with the British battleships and one or both of them were torpedoed by enemy submarine, it would naturally be put down to his absence. That, however, must be risked. In less than ten minutes he had made up his mind, and he led his destroyers round to starboard for the enemy. One of Nelson's sayings was that no Captain could do very wrong if he steered to close the enemy, and Captain Vian had the same idea.

He hoisted the signal for full speed. But it was soon found that full speed could not be maintained in the heavy sea that was running, even though the ships were stern to wind. They were

138

yawing wildly from side to side and were in constant danger of broaching to and being swamped. Green seas were scouring the upper decks, endangering the guns' crews. One man was washed overboard and others were being swept off their feet and injured against the ship's structure. Captain Vian had to reduce to 27 knots, and even at that speed it was hard work to keep the ships under control.

That the enemy was a long way ahead of the Commander-in-Chief was only too evident to the latter. Relieved as he was that the *Bismarck* had been sighted, her reported position confirmed his worst fears that the move to the north-eastward on the day before had lost him vital ground. The Swordfish shadowing reports showed that the enemy was a good thirty miles more to the south-eastward than the Catalina had indicated. On the direct course for Brest, therefore, the *Bismarck* had a lead of about fifty miles over the *King George V*. But this course was not the decisive one. What counted more was the *Bismarck's* quickest course to get under German air cover ; and for this purpose her lead was more like 100 miles, since she could afford not to point as high as Brest itself but could make for the centre of the Bay.

Could the *King George V* overhaul her before she got within comfortable German bomber range? If the *Bismarck* maintained her present reported speed of round about 20 knots, she could be within that range by daylight the next day. To be sure of dealing with her, therefore, it would be necessary to bring her to action before dark : and to do this the *King George V* would have to gain 100 miles on her in eleven hours. At the *Bismarck's* present speed, this was out of the question. The position, in fact, was this ; that if the *Bismarck* were to be brought to action at all, her speed would have to be considerably reduced—down to 15 knots at least—and that the reduction must take place on this day, the 26th.

But how could this be done? Only by torpedoes. The major hope lay in the *Ark Royal's* aircraft. Sir John Tovey knew without being told that Sir James Somerville would use the *Ark Royal* to the full for this purpose. That could be taken for granted. There were also Captain Vian's destroyers, who might get in some night attacks. Sir John was convinced that Captain Vian was already on the way to the enemy with that end in view.[1] But it was a somewhat long chance at the best. Modern ships could take quite a number of torpedoes without losing a great deal of speed; and the *Bismarck* was absolutely brand new.

Vice-Admiral Somerville was, in fact, already planning a torpedo strike. But first of all the ten aircraft sent out on search at 8.40 a.m. had to be got back, refuelled and armed up. By twelve o'clock the aircraft were beginning to return, each one reporting its number by lamp as it got close. All were soon circling overhead except the two who were in touch with the enemy and were staying on until relieved. The real difficulty would be the landing-on. With the stern of the *Ark Royal* being thrown up and down through the height of a house, the aircraft's final approach for the touch-down was obviously going to be a most delicate and hazardous operation. And so it proved. Sometimes, the deck would fall away from under an aircraft just at the critical moment, and compel it to open quickly up and circle round for another try. Only once, fortunately, did the opposite happen, when the deck swung violently upward underneath an incoming aircraft to break it in pieces; the bits having to be pushed overboard before the landing-on could proceed. By good judgment and luck all the other aircraft managed to come down successfully.

The two Swordfish in contact with the enemy had still to come back, but relief shadowers with long-range tanks and specially experienced observers were already on the way. It was, of course, essential that the enemy ship be kept under continuous observation, and relays of shadowers were organized by the *Ark Royal* for the whole of the day.

The resighting of the enemy at 10.30 a.m. had shown Sir James Somerville that his Force H was practically right ahead of the *Bismarck*. What was Sir James to do? He could probably

[1] Sir John Tovey's staff had suggested that he should tell Captain Vian by signal to make for the *Bismarck*. Sir John told them it was unnecessary, that he knew Vian would go for the *Bismarck* and, once in contact, would not let go.

bring the *Bismarck* to action with the *Renown* in less than an hour. Should he do so? In fact, he had no such intention. He had long before decided that the *Renown* was unfit to engage the *Bismarck* alone, though if everything else failed, he was prepared to try a combined attempt with the *Ark Royal's* aircraft. But with the *King George V* and *Rodney* still in the hunt, a single ship action by the *Renown* seemed quite unjustifiable. The Admiralty had also realized that only Force H now stood between the *Bismarck* and harbour, and someone there was evidently apprehensive that Sir James Somerville might get the *Renown* blown up in trying to stop her: for, very shortly after the resighting of the enemy, Admiral Somerville received an Admiralty signal ordering that the *Renown* was not to engage the *Bismarck* unless the latter were already heavily engaged with *King George V* or *Rodney*. If, then, he had to rule out a gun battle, the only alternative was for Sir James to assume a suitable position within convenient aircraft range of the *Bismarck*, for attacks by the *Ark Royal's* Swordfish.

In the choice of such a position, a number of considerations were involved. The position needed to be close to the enemy in order to reduce the flying time to and from the attack, thus enabling more attacks to be delivered in a given period. Conversely, it had to be far enough away to ensure that the *Ark Royal* remained well out of sight and gun range, since a carrier in a gun action is the most vulnerable class of ship afloat, being hardly fit to stand up to a destroyer and 'easy meat' for a cruiser or above.

But to keep a carrier out of this danger while at the same time reasonably close to the target ship is none too straightforward, for the reason that, whenever she is flying off or landing on her aircraft, she is compelled to steer head to wind. The flying off is usually a quick proceeding, the already ranged aircraft following each other off in quick succession. Flying on is liable to be much more protracted. Only one aircraft can come down at a time and it must be struck down on the lifts before the next one lands on. An aircraft may crash, in which case the wreckage must be disposed of before landing on can continue; while if any aircraft makes a bad shot and has to go round for another attempt, this again delays everybody. It is therefore impossible to be certain how long the landing on of a number of aircraft will take. Under difficult conditions, it may well take twenty minutes or more, during all of which time the carrier must be steaming religiously into the wind.

It can therefore be appreciated that in choosing a position for carrier operations against a powerful enemy, the direction of the wind relative to the enemy's course will be an important factor. In this case, the enemy was steaming almost directly down wind. A position to avoid at all costs, therefore, was one directly ahead of him since, when landing on, the carrier would be committed to steering straight towards the advancing enemy ship; and if the process should happen to be unduly prolonged, she might find herself running into gun range and consequent destruction. Conversely, an astern position might lead to the carrier getting too far away to carry out more than one attack.

In these circumstances, the best position was somewhere on the flank, chosen so that the carrier, however long she steamed head to wind, would pass well clear to one side or other of the enemy. The position itself could not be a fixed one. When flying on or off was taking place, the *Ark Royal* and *Bismarck* would be steaming in opposite directions, and unless the former did something to recover the ground she would lose during these periods, she would fairly quickly fall astern. To avoid this, she would have to make a high-speed dash down wind in between flying operations to regain her former place.

The main choice before Sir James Somerville was between the north-eastern and the south-western flanks of the *Bismarck*. He chose the north-eastern, and manœuvred to reach a position about fifty miles on that side of the enemy.

As soon as the aircraft of the morning sweep were back on board the *Ark Royal* and struck down, every available aircraft other than those needed for shadowing was prepared for the coming torpedo strike. The crews had their lunch and came up to the Observer's office to discuss the coming attack. By 2.15 p.m., the fifteen aircraft available for the strike were coming up on the lifts. At 2.40 engines were started up, and at 2.50 the

May 26th

fly-off had begun.[1] The crews had been briefed to attack the *Bismarck* with torpedoes in a position about forty miles in such-and-such a direction. They were told she would be found all by herself on the ocean, no other ship being anywhere near.

At one o'clock Sir James Somerville had made a general signal that the torpedo striking force would leave the *Ark Royal* at three o'clock, and at 3.20 p.m. he made another signal that it had gone off at the time previously mentioned. On board the Home Fleet ships pressing south-eastward, the latter information was received with great satisfaction. Despite the rotten weather, the air attack was on the way. With any luck, the *Bismarck* would be severely damaged and perhaps slowed up enough to be overhauled. With any luck. But mixed with hopefulness was a certain nervous suspense. So much depended on this attack. If it failed, the casualties among the aircraft might be too heavy for another attack to be effective; while it seemed in any case doubtful whether a second attack would succeed if the first did not.

The *Rodney* had just been sighted from the *King George V* slightly before the port beam. Nothing had been heard of her for thirty hours, and now this old 16-in. gun warrior had come silently up over the horizon as if she knew exactly when to take her cue out of the wings. She was 7 knots slower than either the *King George V* or *Bismarck*. Yet here she was making her appearance just where and when she was wanted. During the next few hours she slowly converged on the *King George V*, and by 6 p.m. had formed astern of her. As she drew near, the Admiral had asked her by signal what speed she would do and the reply was 22 knots. The Admiral therefore hoisted the signal for this, and the *King George V's* speed was reduced accordingly, so that the two ships could remain in company. But after about twenty minutes, a signal came across from the *Rodney*: 'I am afraid your 22 knots is a bit faster than ours.' As Sir John Tovey remarked, you could almost hear the old ship panting for breath as she sent the message. The *Rodney* had now only two out of her original three destroyers with her, and they were very short of

[1] One aircraft returned soon after taking off.

143

fuel. Their leader, the *Somali*, had already gone from this cause and had meant to take the others with her. But they, a little fuller, had begged to remain as long as possible and Captain Caslon had let them.

To those who knew what fateful issues were involved, the wait for news of the air attack on the *Bismarck* seemed endless. The aircraft should have been dropping their torpedoes certainly by four o'clock; but that hour passed, and the next, and the next after that in silence that grew increasingly ominous. Had something gone wrong? At half-past six the blow fell. A signal came in from Sir James Somerville that the striking force had scored no hits.

Sir James Somerville, understandably, did not care to say at this juncture why there had been none. The weather had been deteriorating all day, and while the air strike was still in the preparation stage, Sir James had found himself wondering whether the shadowing aircraft could long continue their work. He therefore determined to send the *Sheffield* on ahead to establish a surface contact. About half-past one, more than an hour before the striking force took off, he had ordered her to find and shadow the *Bismarck*. The order was flashed by signal searchlight, and went only to the *Sheffield*.[1] The *Ark Royal*, though in sight of the *Sheffield*, was a mile or two away from her and at the moment was busy flying on some shadowing aircraft. As previously indicated, this was an exciting and absorbing affair, tending to inattention to events in other directions. The visibility was none too good, and there were frequent rainsqualls. When therefore the *Sheffield* put on speed and slipped away towards the *Bismarck*, the *Ark Royal* never noticed her departure. As the *Sheffield* drew out to starboard, Sir James Somerville sent out a wireless signal to the Admiralty, 'repeated for information' to the *Ark Royal*, saying that the *Sheffield* had been sent off to shadow.

---

[1] Sir James Somerville was in his plotting-room discussing the situation with his staff when he ordered the signal to be made to the *Sheffield*. He had it in mind at the time that it would go out by a method which would ensure its reception by the *Ark Royal*. He is, however, of the opinion, which he has expressed to the author, that he should personally have made more sure that it had reached her.

May 26th

When the striking force flew off a little later, the crews believed, as they had been told, that any ship they saw near the position given would be the enemy. Flying through rain and mist, they picked up a ship on their radar sets in roughly the expected position. Going down to have a look, they saw a ship some way ahead. Naturally assuming it was the *Bismarck*, they went back into cloud until it was time to dive to the attack. Then down they went, intent on the assault, their minds fixed on the assured anticipation of seeing the *Bismarck* below them as they broke cloud cover.

It was, in fact, the *Sheffield*. But it was hardly surprising that, in that tense moment, they should fail to recognize her when they came into the open. She was actually their customary training target and they had made many dummy attacks on her in previous months. But they went down expecting to see an enemy, and such is the power of suggestion that it was as an enemy that most of them saw her.

More than an hour after the Swordfish had taken off from the *Ark Royal*, her signal officer had hurried up to Captain Maund with a copy of a signal that had just been deciphered. It was the wireless message from Vice-Admiral Somerville to the Admiralty, repeated for information to the *Ark Royal*, saying that the *Sheffield* had gone ahead to shadow. It had been on board the *Ark Royal* since about 2 p.m., but had only just been dealt with by the cipher staff. The reason for the delay was that a great many signals were flowing in for deciphering at this time, including those from the *Ark Royal's* own aircraft who were reporting the *Bismarck* every few minutes, and the cipher staff were hard-pressed by the volume of the traffic. A signal, therefore, which was not addressed directly to but only marked as repeated to the ship was taken as being of secondary importance and was put aside for a quiet moment. When its turn did come to be attended to, its significance was immediately appreciated: hence the signal officer's anxious concern as he came to his Captain.

Captain Maund as instantly perceived the grave implications of the signal. He decided at once that heroic measures were justifiable in the endeavour to avoid a ghastly error. Throwing

K 145

secrecy to the winds in order to gain time, he made a signal in plain language to the striking force to 'look out for *Sheffield*'. But it was too late.

When the *Sheffield* had been detached to find and shadow the *Bismarck*, Captain Larcom had had the frequent reports from the shadowing aircraft to guide him to the spot. How far away from her he was when the Swordfish were approaching him is uncertain, but he had not actually sighted her. He had received Sir James Somerville's signals that the air striking force would be coming and that it had taken off at 3 p.m. He was therefore expecting to have the Swordfish fly over him, and it was with no surprise that it was reported to him about a quarter to four that they were in sight. As he turned his glasses on to them, however, he suddenly realized after a moment or two of incredulity, that they were diving down to attack his ship. Instantly, he rang down for full speed and put his wheel over to confuse the attackers' aim. Not a gun was fired by the *Sheffield*, and her officers and men watched in silence the released torpedoes dropping towards the water, intended for them.

The first fell into the sea with a heavy splash, and the impotent observers braced themselves for an approaching torpedo track. A moment later their attention was focused by something even more arresting. The second torpedo reached the sea, but as it touched the water it detonated with a thunderous roar, flinging a fountain of spray in all directions. The next torpedo did the same thing. Before starting, the torpedo heads had been armed with magnetic pistols, and it was plain that these were going off on hitting the water. Of the remaining torpedoes, three more exploded innocuously in this manner well away from the *Sheffield*. Three aircraft moreover realized as they dived down that a mistake was being made, and withheld their torpedoes. Thus, there were only six or seven dangerous torpedoes for the *Sheffield* to contend with. By this time she was swinging rapidly round at high speed. With every spare officer and man on the bridge scanning the sea for the tell-tale tracks, Captain Larcom swung the ship one way and another to avoid the torpedoes, and with such skill that all passed him harmlessly by.

It was a gloomy set of airmen that returned to the carrier. They had set out with such high hopes; all the higher because Fleet Air Arm had still to win an established reputation in sea warfare, and the young men of the *Ark Royal* were longing to set a lustrous example for others to follow. But all they had achieved was this lamentable anti-climax of attacking a friendly ship. Until they were back on board, Captain Maund did not become aware of the distressing story that had to be told. But he, knowing it was not the aircrews' fault, told them not to worry and that they would have another chance a little later. They were to go down and get something to eat, and then come up to discuss the next attack. Under this sympathetic treatment, their misery fell away and was replaced, as Captain Maund could see, by a grim determination not to have any further mishaps.

To Sir John Tovey, the signal that the air striking force had scored no hits was bitter news. He did not know that the aircraft had attacked the wrong ship. In ignorance of that fact, he naturally assumed that the attack had been made against the *Bismarck* and had been a complete failure. Either, he supposed, the weather had been too bad or the *Bismarck's* flak had been too fierce or her avoiding tactics too skilful; or a combination of these factors had been too much for the attackers.

Whatever the cause, the implications of the failure were thoroughly depressing. In announcing the lack of any hits, Sir James Somerville had said that another striking force would leave the *Ark Royal* at 6.30 p.m. But Sir John Tovey could not be too sanguine about its prospects of success. The first attack having given completely negative results, there could be very little reason for expecting anything startling from the second. One or two hits might possibly be got, but it would be fatuously optimistic to hope that the *Bismarck* would be decisively slowed up. The next attack would presumably be the last that day, and if it left her speed unaffected she would certainly be out of reach by the morning. This was virtually the last chance of a slow-up by air attack, and it would be almost a miracle if it came off. Destroyer night attacks offered a further hope, but it was to be feared a somewhat slender one. Night attacks on single ships were not very promising even in fine weather, and the present conditions of gale, high seas and rain-squalls were about as unpropitious as they could be.

Sir John found himself compelled to face the possibility, indeed the probability, that the *Bismarck* would not be slowed up that night. And if she were not, he knew that he had a very unpleasant decision to make. It would be that he himself must give up the hunt. For the last twenty-four hours or so, he and his staff had been keeping a close and increasingly anxious watch on the fuel situation. The *King George V* was now down to 32 per cent of her total capacity, with the journey home still to do; while the *Rodney* had just reported that she could only remain till 8 a.m. the next morning.

Nor was it merely that enough fuel had to be retained to take the ships back to harbour. They also needed to preserve a sufficiently high speed for dealing with enemy submarine or air attack. It could be taken for granted that German submarines had been concentrating in these waters for several days, and heavy air attack was to be expected before long.[1] To have only low speed available when undergoing either forms of attack would add greatly to its danger.

To run this risk was not necessarily to ensure the *Bismarck's* destruction. She might still get into harbour, and the *King George V* nevertheless be sunk through inability to steam fast. This would be a calamity of the first order. With the *Hood* gone and the *Prince of Wales* damaged, the *King George V* was at the moment the only battleship strong and fast enough to compete with the *Bismarck*; while the *Tirpitz* might also be at sea before long. In these circumstances, there was an obvious limit to the hazards to which the *King George V* could legitimately be exposed, and

---

[1] Because the Germans had expected the *Bismarck* to be lost in the Atlantic for some time, they had made no arrangements to station submarines in the approaches to Brest to cover her possible retreat thither. They did recall submarines from convoy hunting when the emergency arose, but a number of the U-boats that obeyed the call had already fired all their torpedoes. At 8 p.m. on 26th May, U566 (Lieut. Wohlfarth) could have had a sitting shot at the *Renown* and *Ark Royal* which passed him at close range on a straight course. But he had nothing to fire at them. The Germans also sent U-boats out from Brest, but these combed the wrong area, sighting neither the *Bismarck* nor any British ships.

148

May 26th

Sir John Tovey was by now painfully aware that the limit had almost been reached. Unless the situation changed radically for the better in the next few hours, the *King George V* would have to turn back. Sir John saw very little chance, however, that the situation would so improve. About 6.20 p.m., therefore, he despatched a signal to tell Sir James Somerville—which would also be taken in by the Admiralty—that unless the enemy's speed had been reduced by midnight, the *King George V* would turn back then to refuel. The *Rodney* could continue the pursuit a little longer, though without her destroyers.

It was an agonizing signal for Sir John Tovey to have to send out. He had chased the *Bismarck* for four days and nights, covering more than 2,000 miles in the process, and following her from the fringe of the Arctic Circle almost to the Bay of Biscay. To turn back without bringing her to action would be heart-rending. Moreover, it was his job to prevent such a break-out as the *Bismarck* was attempting and looked like bringing off; and whatever the cause, he would never quite forgive himself if she were to escape into port.

CHAPTER 9

A Last-Minute Transformation

After emerging safely from the disconcerting episode of the Swordfish attack, the *Sheffield* had gone on to find the *Bismarck*. On her bridge, everyone was scanning the horizon ahead for a sign of a ship, and the lookouts had been promised two pounds to the first man to sight her. At 5.40 p.m., the officer of the watch said: 'I think I can see something on the port bow.' All binoculars were raised to look in that direction and, sure enough, a dim grey shape could just be made out on the misty horizon. Was it the *Bismarck*? At first it was difficult to say, but as the *Sheffield* came closer the silhouette of the *Bismarck* became unmistakable. Once again, a shadowing warship was in contact after an interval of more than a day and a half.

Captain Larcom did not want to be seen if it could be avoided, and he altered course away and began to work round to get astern of the enemy at a distance of seven to ten miles. He began also to send in the usual shadower's reports of the enemy's position, course and speed. These reports were supplementing those going out from the *Ark Royal's* shadowing aircraft who, in successive pairs, had been keeping a continuous watch on the *Bismarck* since 11.15 a.m.

For short periods, one of the Coastal Command Catalinas also took a hand. Z /209, the original sighter of the *Bismarck*, had lost touch with her before eleven o'clock, and though she remained searching for another four hours, she never regained it. Her consort, M /240, was ordered to close and assist in the

150

shadowing as soon as Z /209's first sighting report came through. This other Catalina succeeded in finding the *Bismarck* for short periods at half-past one and again at four o'clock. Unfortunately, on both these occasions, she and the shadowing Swordfish viewed each other with grave suspicion. Reporting that she was being attacked by enemy aircraft, M /240 twice took avoiding action and lost contact, the second time for good. At the same time, the Swordfish, believing that a Focke-Wulf had appeared on the scene, nipped into the clouds for cover, though luckily without more than momentary loss of touch with the *Bismarck*. A further complication was that the Catalina's reports of the enemy's position, when signalled, differed by sixty miles from those emanating from the Swordfish and the *Sheffield*.

Whether or not the *Bismarck* could see the *Sheffield*, she made no hostile move. Possibly she felt that, as she was obviously being reported by aircraft, it would serve no useful purpose and be only a waste of ammunition to try to drive away the cruiser, anyway during daylight.

Meanwhile, feverish activity was going on in the *Ark Royal* to get the next striking force ready to go. There was no time to be lost and everyone was working at top speed. With the ship rolling heavily, aircraft were refuelled and more torpedoes got ready. One lesson at least of immediate practical value had been learnt from the attack on the *Sheffield*. The magnetic pistols were unreliable. Captain Maund, therefore, decided to substitute for the next attack the old and well-tried contact pistols, which fired only when they hit something. Their use raised the question of what depth setting to give the torpedoes. With magnetic pistols this was no problem, since the torpedoes had only to be set deep enough to run underneath the target ship. But if they had actually to hit her, the question was how far down? Ideally, the deeper the better; but the present weather introduced a very awkward unknown factor into the calculations. In heavy weather, with waves running high, torpedoes are liable to behave very erratically in regard to depth-keeping and are known to dive well below their intended depth setting. As impact was now essential, it was therefore decided to set the torpedoes for the comparatively shallow depth of ten feet, in the hope that this would keep them always above the *Bismarck's* keel.

This time, too, there would be no mistake about the *Sheffield*. To make assurance extra sure, the aircraft were told to conact that ship on their way to the *Bismarck*, and the *Sheffield* herself was told that they would do so.

By 7 p.m. the striking force was up on deck and ranged. There were fifteen Swordfish, every single torpedo-bomber that remained in the ship. It was still blowing hard. Visibility was exceedingly variable, cloud was at about 600 feet or less, and rainstorms covering very large areas were sweeping across the sea. Once more the ship was turned into the wind and once more the aircraft careered unsteadily along the heaving deck before they rose clear into storm-swept sky. As they formed up in the air and disappeared in the direction of the enemy, everyone in the *Ark Royal* knew that they meant to succeed this time.

About forty minutes later, just before 8 p.m., the *Sheffield* sighted them coming. She made to them 'the enemy is twelve miles dead ahead', and they were seen climbing into the clouds. Half an hour later they were back to ask for another bearing, having apparently failed to find the *Bismarck*. Redirected, they departed once more in the enemy's direction. There was too much rain and low cloud about for the *Sheffield's* people to keep them long in sight. But after an interval there came an outburst of gunfire fine on the starboard bow and the bright winking of numerous shell bursts in the air which showed plainly that the attack was starting.

The distant display of anti-aircraft fire flashed and sparkled away for some minutes and then died away. There was a pause, and then those on the bridge of the *Sheffield* saw first one and then two more Swordfish flying towards them. They came past very low on a level with the bridge. It could be seen that their torpedoes had gone, and as one Swordfish flew by very close the crew were smiling broadly and had their thumbs held upwards. All those on the *Sheffield's* bridge and upper deck took off their caps and gave them a cheer as they passed.

May 26th

The attacks went on, and owing to the bad weather conditions were somewhat protracted. Mostly, the *Sheffield* could see little of what was happening, but at times, in a clear patch, her people saw the *Bismarck* spurting flame from every anti-aircraft gun, while through binoculars it was occasionally possible to spot some of the aircraft as they dived down and flattened out low over the water to drop their torpedoes.

Had the day been fine and clear, a simultaneous assault by the whole force would doubtless have been delivered. As it was, on nearing the enemy's position the aircraft encountered a thick bank of cloud, rising 6,000 to 10,000 feet above its base a few hundred feet from the sea. Inside this cloud bank the striking force got split up. Some aircraft went straight on at the same level till they reached what they estimated to be the correct attacking point. Others spent time in climbing several thousand feet before diving down. Those that did this experienced varying degrees of icing. On breaking cloud cover, some aircraft did not find the enemy where expected and had either to work round in the open or go back into cloud for another approach. One pair and one single aircraft lost the enemy completely and separately went back to the *Sheffield* for redirection. One aircraft found the flak so heavy that it gave up the attack and jettisoned its torpedoes before returning to the carrier. Altogether, the attacks were spread out over about half an hour, from 8.55 p.m. to 9.25 p.m.

While the attacks were still proceeding, those on the *Sheffield's* bridge noticed that the *Bismarck* was altering course. She would naturally swerve about a good deal to dodge the torpedoes being dropped at her. Now she was getting almost broadside on to the *Sheffield*. Then suddenly from the distant enemy ship there came four rippling yellow flashes from her turret guns. As if stung to fury by the air attacks against her, she had opened fire on the only British ship she could see.

The shells fell a long way, perhaps more than a mile, from the *Sheffield*; and someone on her bridge made a derisory remark about the shooting. He spoke too soon. Again the enemy's turrets spurted their bright tongues of flame, and about fifty

153

A Last-Minute Transformation

seconds later there were some piercing cracks as four 15-in. shells fell very close on either side of the British cruiser, exploding on hitting the water. Huge splashes shot up alongside, and the air was filled with whizzing shell splinters. Captain Larcom went on to full speed, put the wheel over to get clear, and gave the order to make smoke. But before that last order had produced any result four more enemy salvoes had fallen unpleasantly close.

The splinters from the second one had caused casualties among the anti-aircraft gun crews, twelve men being wounded, three of whom died. They had also destroyed the ship's radar apparatus, an awkward piece of damage, as it meant the *Sheffield* could now only shadow by eyesight, and would therefore be ineffective for that purpose after dark.

It was a hectic few minutes, with the sudden outburst of shell-fire, the hurried giving of orders, the frantic rolling of the ship as she came beam on to the sea, the swish and smack of the incoming spray and the rising howl of the gale as she turned at high speed into the wind; and at last, none too soon, the dense volumes of jet-black smoke pouring out of the funnels, blotting out the *Sheffield* from the vicious enemy's sight. The moments had been too crowded for a calm and leisurely observation of the *Bismarck's* behaviour. But she had been seen to continue her turn into the wind. As he swung round away from her gun-fire, Captain Larcom ordered a signal to go out that she was steering 340° (NNW.). What had been the *Bismarck's* game? Had she thought this was a good moment to drive away her one surface shadower before dark, when the air attacks were in any case compelling her to twist and turn? Or was there some other explanation? Captain Larcom could not tell.

Many miles below the horizon, Sir John Tovey had even less means of knowing. All he had to go on was Captain Larcom's report that the *Bismarck* had almost reversed her course. What did it mean? In view of the shattering signal just previously received from the leader of the attacking aircraft it probably meant nothing. This signal had been short and very much to the point. It said: 'Estimate no hits.' It was assumed by the Admiral and indeed by all ships that took it in, that the signal referred to the

154

attack as a whole and indicated that, like its predecessor, it had been a complete failure.[1] The gloom thereby engendered was naturally abysmal. Captain Dalrymple-Hamilton told his ship's company over the loudspeakers that no hits had been obtained and added that he very much feared there was now no hope of bringing the *Bismarck* to action. Commodore Blackman of the *Edinburgh* reached the same conclusion. He had been in sight of the *King George V* and *Rodney*, off and on, since early in the day. At about 5 p.m. he had crossed astern of them to make straight for the *Bismarck's* reported position. But though he ran across both *Sheffield* and *Ark Royal* at different times and therefore must have got very close to the *Bismarck* herself, he did not succeed in sighting her. By this time, his fuel position was verging on the desperate, and the report that the second air attack had gained no hits decided him to give up the pursuit. He turned his ship for home.

To Sir John Tovey the 'no hits' signal was the culminating rebuff. All was now clearly over. The *Bismarck* was practically certain to get away and there would be little left for him, Sir John, to do but to make his mournful way back to his base. As for the *Sheffield's* report, it was quite obvious what that was. She had made the common mistake of estimating the enemy's course 180 degrees wrong. He remarked a little sourly to his staff that she must have 'joined the reciprocal club'.[2]

He had hardly said it when another signal was brought to him. It was from one of the shadowing aircraft and it said that the *Bismarck* was steering due north. As he read it, Sir John realized at once that the *Sheffield* had been right after all. It was conceivable that she could have misjudged the *Bismarck's* course by 180 degrees; but surely not that she and a shadowing aircraft

---

[1] The rain, gale, and low clouds had caused the aircraft of the striking force to lose touch with each other and to attack in scattered units. The squadron leader was among the first to go down to the attack and had with him only a fraction of the force. He seems to have assumed that the remainder had lost the target for good and all; and since he thought his own party had obtained no hits, he evidently imagined that there would be no hits at all. So he made a signal to that effect.

[2] Naval slang for the erroneous reporting of the reciprocal of the real inclination or bearing. It is not a difficult mistake to make in regard to a distant ship nearly end-on, the stern of a warship being almost as sharp as its bows.

could both have done it simultaneously. The *Bismarck* had undoubtedly turned right round. But this did not necessarily mean a great deal. Such a turn, drastic though it was, was not incompatible with the frustrating of an aircraft attack. The next report would surely show the *Bismarck* as back to east-south-east. But the next report, nine minutes later, did not. It made her still steering north-north-west. Another nine minutes passed, and again an aircraft report was handed to the Commander-in-Chief. Again it said that the *Bismarck* was heading about north-north-west. Sir John and his staff looked at each other with bewildered hopefulness. Could it really be true that the *Bismarck*, for no apparent reason, was steaming back on her tracks? Then, five minutes later, there came a second report from the *Sheffield*, in which the enemy's course was given as north.

There was now no room for doubt. The *Bismarck* was clearly moving in a general northward direction. But if she had not been hit, why was she behaving in this strange, and indeed suicidal, manner? It was to her vital interest to make every mile of progress she could towards the south-east. Yet here she was steering almost in the opposite direction for nearly half an hour. Was it possible that she had been hit after all? The thought was forming among Sir John Tovey and his staff that the *Bismarck's* otherwise inexplicable movements might be due to her rudders being damaged and she herself being no longer under control.

Whatever the explanation, the situation had turned dramatically in the British favour. If the *Bismarck* was heading northwards, even temporarily, it meant that Sir John Tovey's force would be closing her at the rate of from 30 to 45 knots, according to her speed. This was a change of fortune which it would never do to ignore. What exactly had happened to the *Bismarck*, Sir John could only guess; but if by any wonderful chance she were to continue in a northerly direction, there would be the possibility of an action before nightfall. In any case, her interesting conduct was worth investigating, and two minutes after the *Sheffield's* second report reaching him Sir John led round to a course of south, directly towards the *Bismarck's* position.

The *Sheffield* was still steering northward to open the range from the *Bismarck*, and just before ten o'clock she sighted some destroyers coming down from the north-westward. These were Captain Vian's five ships who had been steaming hard to overtake the *Bismarck* for the previous nine hours. They had already seen the *Renown* in the distance[1] and had in turn been sighted by the *Ark Royal's* aircraft on their way back from the attack. The sun was getting low towards the horizon. Yet even in the evening light, the destroyers made an inspiring spectacle as they came racing up, yawing about and heeling far over as they tore along down wind, the white of their foaming bow waves prominent even among the breaking seas. As they neared the *Sheffield*, Captain Vian asked her for the bearing of the *Bismarck*, and, receiving it, swept past and onwards toward the enemy.

The air striking force had begun to return to the *Ark Royal* at about 9 p.m., but they had a long way to go, and the last of them was not on board till an hour and a half later. Five had been damaged by gunfire. In one 127 holes were counted, the pilot and air gunner having both been wounded. But despite all this and the failing light, only one aircraft crashed.

It was a more cheerful lot of airmen who climbed out of their aircraft and went up to tell their stories. The crews were interrogated separately as they returned, and it was not until well after 10 p.m. that Captain Maund felt satisfied that one hit had been obtained amidships on the *Bismarck*. He signalled this over by lamp to Vice-Admiral Somerville, who passed it out by wireless at approximately 10.30 p.m. This report did not clarify the situation very much. If the hit had actually been amidships, it would be most unlikely to have been responsible for the *Bismarck's* northerly course. Nevertheless, the report sufficed to bring the *Edinburgh* back towards the enemy. Since the *Bismarck* had been hit after all, there might now be an early engagement; and if so Commodore Blackman was going to be there. How he was to manage for fuel he hardly dared to think. It crossed his mind that he might have to put in at a Southern Irish

---

[1] Actually, *Piorun* was the only destroyer sighted by *Renown*. Vice-Admiral Somerville had dictated a signal telling the senior officer to shadow and attack as opportunity offered. But when he discovered that Captain Vian was in command, he decided the signal was unnecessary.

port, though he was uncertain how the Eire Government interpreted its obligations as a neutral.

Meanwhile, darkness had been coming on, and Sir John Tovey knew that the air shadowers would soon have to return to the *Ark Royal*. But he also knew that, thanks to Captain Vian's initiative earlier in the day, the latter's destroyers were now in the *Bismarck's* vicinity and would presumably soon be taking over the watch.[1] To assist them in gaining contact, Sir John asked Vice-Admiral Somerville if the air shadowers could guide the destroyers to the enemy, and this instruction was passed to them via the *Ark Royal*. They seem to have left the *Bismarck* at about 10 p.m. and made a sweep in search of the destroyers. These they eventually found, but had by that time become too 'lost' themselves to act as guides. Just before 10.30 p.m. they were recalled to the *Ark Royal*.

But Captain Vian was taking his destroyers in the right direction, and at ten minutes to eleven, after a silence of about three-quarters of an hour, the other British forces were cheered by a contact signal from the *Zulu*, showing that the destroyers were in touch. By now, Sir John Tovey was convinced that the *Bismarck* had been injured in such a way as to prevent her maintaining a continuous south-easterly course and to compel her frequently to come round head to wind, which by good fortune was blowing from the north-west. He was satisfied that she could not now escape him; and he therefore decided that, as night was falling, he would not seek an action at once but would wait for daylight. The positions of the enemy and of other British forces were none too certain and there was always the chance of an unfortunate incident if one of the latter was met unexpectedly in the darkness. At 11.36 p.m. Sir John altered course to about north-north-east to work round to the northward and westward of the *Bismarck*, with the object of having her silhouetted against the early morning light when he made his attack. He had hardly got round to his course when he received another signal from Vice-Admiral Somerville to say there had

---

[1] Sir John Tovey had intercepted a signal from the *Renown* saying that the destroyers had been seen passing her at 7 p.m.

probably been a second hit on the *Bismarck*, on her starboard quarter. Apparently, the signal was written out at 2240 (10.40 p.m.) since it bore that time of origin. But it was an hour later when it was received in the *King George V.*

The word 'quarter' was highly significant,[1] and indeed was the sort of evidence for which they had all been waiting for two hours and a half. A hit on the quarter might well mean that the *Bismarck's* propellors or rudder or both had been damaged, rendering her unmanageable. Sir John Tovey felt more confident than ever that he now had her at his mercy, and he made a signal that she appeared severely damaged and that he would be engaging from the westward at dawn. He also wrote a message to Captain Patterson, wishing the flagship good luck and victory in the coming fight.[2]

Unwittingly, however, Sir John was evidently causing some perturbation at the Admiralty. His north-north-easterly course, which he had announced by signal shortly after altering to it at 11.36 p.m., happened to be the course for the United Kingdom; and since he had previously signalled that unless the enemy were substantially slowed up he would turn back at midnight, someone at the Admiralty seems to have jumped to the conclusion that Sir John had actually done so. For there came shortly afterwards a slightly agitated signal from Whitehall saying that Sir John had said his course was north-north-east and was he still in the chase?

The Admiral's alteration of course told Commodore Blackman of the *Edinburgh* that he now had no chance of being in at the finish. To wait till daylight was out of the question if he was to get back to harbour. Once more he turned for home, this time for good, and steaming at economical speed eventually reached Londonderry with 5½ per cent of fuel in his tanks.

Meanwhile, the last aircraft shadowers had just got back to the *Ark Royal* with practically no petrol left, and in spite of the darkness and the lively pitching of the ship had somehow

---

[1] The quarter is that part of a ship about halfway between the middle of her length and the stern.

[2] See the following page.

managed to make a successful landing. The crews had some important information to impart. It was that immediately after the aircraft attack the *Bismarck* had made two complete circles and had apparently come to a stop heading north, on which point of the compass she lay wallowing in the seas. This was the final link in the evidence needed to complete the whole chain.

To. K.G.V.

The sinking of the Bismarck may have an effect on the War, as a whole out of all proportion to the loss to the enemy of one battleship.

May God be with you and grant you victory.

J. . 26/5/41

Captain Maund flashed it over at once to the *Renown*, and Admiral Somerville sent it on to Sir John Tovey by wireless at a minute before one o'clock, with a time of origin of 0046 (12.46 a.m.).

It was direct and invaluable confirmation of what Sir John had been suspecting for some time. The picture was now indeed reasonably clear to everyone on the British side.[1] After the strain and anxieties of the past few days, culminating in the two wretched disappointments of the previous six hours, when hope of catching the *Bismarck* had declined practically to zero, the enemy's evident disablement seemed almost too good to be true. To the senior officers, particularly, the relief was immense. They, who had known the general strategical situation as their juniors had not, had previously almost despaired of getting the *Bismarck*. They had realized that the air attack which had done the vital damage was virtually the last hope of slowing the *Bismarck* up and thus preventing her escape; and that such a last-minute attempt should be an overwhelming success was beyond reasonable expectation. It was hundreds to one against it happening. Yet, the one forlorn chance had come off. That this astonishing reversal of fortune should have occurred when it did seemed like the direct intervention of Providence.

All that Sir John Tovey now wanted to bring off his dawn attack were reports of the *Bismarck's* position during the night, and these he was confident he would get from Captain Vian's destroyers. A few minutes after receiving the 'circling' signal, he altered course right round to south-west. Sir John had also requested Sir James Somerville to take his Force H not less than twenty miles to the southward of the enemy. That would be quite close enough for the operation of the *Ark Royal's* aircraft, and Sir John Tovey thought it best to keep the *Renown* well clear. An hour or two before, Sir James had suggested bringing her over to join the battleships. But Sir John was anxious to avoid any possibility of mistaking her for the enemy in the darkness, while he believed the *King George V* and *Rodney* quite strong enough for the job in hand.

To the north of the *King George V*, the *Norfolk* was still striving to catch up. She had shortened the distance the battleships were ahead of her during the day, but she was still behind them. Being seriously short of fuel, Captain Phillips had been hesitating

---

[1] '... Until the Flag Officer commanding Force H's 0046 was received, it was not clear that the enemy had suffered a serious reduction of speed.'—Commodore Blackman's dispatch.

A Last-Minute Transformation

to go too fast. But when the last air attack was due to be in progress, he could contain himself no longer. He put the telegraphs to full speed.

Another British warship was now speeding towards the *Bismarck*. Captain B. C. S. Martin of the cruiser *Dorsetshire* had been acting as the escort of Convoy SL74 coming north. At 11 a.m. on the 26th, he and the convoy were about 600 miles west of Cape Finisterre, when the Admiralty's signal was taken in that the *Bismarck* had been sighted just before. The plot of the enemy's position made her 300 miles due north of the *Dorsetshire*, and Captain Martin realized that if the *Bismarck* were making for Brest, he could probably intercept her.

He made up his mind to leave the convoy and steer to meet the enemy. The intercepting course was about east and nearly down wind, which meant that the *Dorsetshire* could maintain a good speed. Captain Martin turned to east-north-east and went on to 26 knots. At 5 p.m., he altered course to east and increased to 28 knots.

CHAPTER 10

The Destroyers Attack at Night

When Captain Vian sighted the *Sheffield* ahead of him just before 10 p.m., his destroyers were spread in line abreast, two and a half miles apart, and the *Sheffield* on the opposite course passed through the line a quarter of an hour later. Learning from her that the *Bismarck* was not far off and when last seen was heading north to north-west, Captain Vian reduced speed. In the growing dusk and with heavy seas running, it might be dangerous to make the final approach too fast. It was expected to sight the *Bismarck* ahead of the centre destroyer. But at 10.38 p.m., she was seen a little on the starboard bow of the port wing ship, the *Piorun*; and shortly after the latter's next-in-line, the *Zulu*, also spotted her and was the first to get off a sighting report.

Within a very few minutes, the *Bismarck* sighted the *Piorun* and opened fire on her with both main and secondary armaments. Undismayed, the tiny *Piorun* returned the fire with her 4.7-in. guns. It is very unlikely that she did any good, and she herself, being frequently straddled, was in grave danger. But it was a most spirited display, and the *Piorun* actually kept up the hopelessly unequal contest for over half an hour before she ceased spitting fire at her armoured antagonist and hauled out of range.

Captain Vian had discovered the enemy he was seeking, and he now had to decide what policy to adopt towards him. As his destroyers drew closer and could make a better estimate of the *Bismarck's* movements, it became apparent that she was

163

The Destroyers Attack at Night

proceeding at low speed and was steering erratically. Captain Vian concluded that interception by the British heavy ships was fairly certain in the morning, if not earlier, provided the enemy were successfully held during the night. He therefore made up his mind that his first duty was to shadow the *Bismarck* with a view to guiding the *King George V* and *Rodney* to her position. He would, however, as a secondary duty, deliver torpedo attacks as opportunities offered, and provided this did not involve heavy losses among his ships.

Immediately after sighting the enemy, he had ordered his destroyers to take up their shadowing positions, and they were moving over to do that now. The *Maori*, *Sikh*, *Zulu*, and *Piorun* were to form a square round the *Bismarck*, one on each bow and one on each quarter; while the *Cossack*, Captain Vian's ship, would shadow from astern. It would take some time for all the destroyers to get into position, especially as the two detailed for the farther positions had to keep out of gun range while reaching them, involving something of a detour.

At about 11.15 p.m., however, the *Bismarck* made things easier by altering course in the destroyers' direction. Since they had first sighted her, she had seemed to be oscillating about a mean course of roughly north-east. She now swung round to about north-north-west. But it was nearly dark; and the outer destroyers did not immediately become aware of the *Bismarck's* alteration, and so went on for a short time in the wrong direction.

At 11.24 p.m., Captain Vian made the signal for taking up preparatory stations for a synchronized torpedo attack. His plan, previously communicated to the other ships, was for three destroyers on one side of the *Bismarck* and for two on the other all to attack together, coming in on both the enemy's bows to fire their torpedoes at the same time. The weather was, however, unfavourable for an organized attack of this kind. It was blowing very hard and there was a big sea running. The destroyers could manage a fair speed down wind, but could make only moderate progress against it. At more than about 18 knots, when anywhere near head to sea, they could hardly see for the spray they threw up as they plunged into the oncoming waves.

164

May 26th

It was a pitch dark night. There was no moon and the blanket of cloud overhead shut out any faint light from the stars. Normally this should have been in the destroyers' favour, for the blacker the night the closer they should have been able to get to the *Bismarck* without being observed; they, the much smaller targets, being due to sight her first.

It very soon became clear, however, that the darkness was no handicap to the *Bismarck*. Time after time, she opened a very accurate fire on the destroyers whether they could see her or not, and therefore she them. She was evidently firing by radar and was consequently independent of visual sighting; and, moreover, she obviously intended to show the destroyers they would approach her at their peril.

The first destroyer to receive her attentions in this way was Captain Vian's own *Cossack*. At 11.42 p.m., while she was still four miles away from the *Bismarck*, flashes of gunfire were seen from the latter's direction, and salvoes of large and small shells fell close alongside the *Cossack*, the splinters from which shot away some of her wireless aerials. The shooting was too good to be trifled with, and the *Cossack* was forced to sheer away.

Eight minutes later, the *Zulu* received the same treatment. She could just make out the *Bismarck* to the northward and had seen her shooting at the *Cossack*. Now the enemy's guns flashed out again; and a few seconds later a 15-in. salvo straddled the *Zulu* herself. Two more similar salvoes straddled her in quick succession, the splinters wounding one officer and two men. It was providential she was not hit and she made haste to turn away and get further off. In this process, she lost touch and did not regain it for more than an hour.

It was the first time in history that radar-controlled gunfire had been used against ships at night; and it was a weird and rather awe-inspiring experience for the destroyers to undergo. Had the *Bismarck* been using searchlights, it would have seemed less unnatural. But there was no such warning. Out of the darkness in the *Bismarck's* direction would come a ripple of brilliant flashes, momentarily lighting up the sky. A ten- or fifteen-seconds' pause, and then the shriek of approaching shells and a quick succession of terrific, splitting cracks, as they hit the water. Simultaneously, a vast upheaval in the sea near the ship and a number of indistinct masses would tower up ghost-like and immense in the darkness alongside. Then another sudden glare of gunfire, momentarily revealing huge columns of cascading water close at hand.

The *Sikh* and *Maori* had been next to each other in the original line-abreast search and were not far apart now. The *Sikh*, the nearer of the two to the *Bismarck*, had lost sight of her in the darkness about half an hour before, but saw her firing at the *Cossack*. Steering in, she picked up the enemy from astern. From this position she shadowed till twenty minutes past midnight, when the *Bismarck* suddenly altered course to port and opened fire on her with full broadside open. Again, the shooting was very unpleasantly accurate. The *Sikh* was reasonably close to the enemy and her Captain gave orders for torpedoes to be fired. But the torpedo control officer's view towards the enemy was so obscured by an intervening curtain of shell splashes that he could not get the necessary data for the torpedo settings, and the *Sikh* had to withdraw without firing.

The *Maori*, near the *Sikh*, came in for some of the overs meant for the latter, but was able to take over the shadowing for a few minutes until she lost touch in the darkness.

For the next half-hour, from half-past twelve till one o'clock in the morning, the *Bismarck* seems to have been unshadowed, all destroyers having lost touch. There was a good deal of excuse. It was an inky-black night and, in addition to the gale and the heavy seas, frequent rain squalls were being encountered, in which the visibility was probably less than half a mile. To lose touch with a darkened ship under these conditions was only too easy.[1]

The *Zulu* had been searching north after being driven away by the enemy's fire at 11.45 p.m., and had just come across the *Cossack* in the darkness; and a little later they both encountered a vessel which turned out to be the *Piorun*. By this time, Captain

---

[1] The author understands that some if not all of the destroyers were fitted with radar, though of an early and not very efficient pattern.

Vian had come to the conclusion that no set-piece attack was possible. The *Bismarck's* ability to keep his ships at a distance by radar-controlled gunfire had made the darkness a handicap rather than an advantage. In escaping from the enemy's broadsides, his destroyers had become scattered. He had just met the *Zulu* and the *Piorun* by chance, but he had no idea of the whereabouts of the *Maori* and *Sikh*. He had no assurance that any of them knew the exact position of the *Bismarck*. He did not know it himself at the moment. If attacks were to be made at all, each destroyer would have to make her own, as best she could. He made a signal at twenty minutes to one that destroyers should attack when opportunities presented themselves.

On receiving this signal, Commander Graham of the *Zulu*, at once went off to the westward by himself. As he did so, a star shell winked out into light on his port bow and began its slow descent to the sea. It was from the *Maori*, who was taking a look in the direction where she had last seen the enemy. But it revealed nothing. At about one o'clock, however, the *Zulu* sighted the black shape of the *Bismarck* on the starboard bow, steering apparently a little west of north. The *Zulu* was right astern of the enemy ship and had to get much farther up on or before her beam in order to fire torpedoes. Commander Graham therefore decided to run up on the *Bismarck's* port side and went on to as high a speed as he could manage. The enemy must have been going very slowly, for it only took the *Zulu* about twenty minutes to get abreast of her, at an estimated range of 5,000 yards. At this point, the *Bismarck* opened a hot fire, and a minute or two later Commander Graham fired all his four torpedoes and then sheered away to open the range. So far as could be judged, none of the torpedoes hit.

The gunfire directed at the *Zulu* showed the *Maori* where the *Bismarck* was, and she steered in that direction. Judging by the gunflashes, the *Maori* was also astern of the *Bismarck*; and Commander Armstrong, like Commander Graham, determined to work forward on the enemy's port side. He got up to a position about 4,000 yards on the *Bismarck's* port beam apparently without being seen. As it was very dark and he wanted to make sure of his aim, Commander Armstrong then fired a star shell to light the enemy up while he attacked; and as soon as it was burning, he fired two torpedoes. This was at 1.37 a.m.

The moment the star shell broke into light, the *Bismarck* opened fire, and as usual made excellent shooting. Immediately after firing his torpedoes, Commander Armstrong had begun to turn towards the enemy. He fancied she was altering course towards him and he thought he would cross her bows and fire his other two torpedoes from her other side. The *Bismarck's* fire was, however, much too fierce, and the *Maori* altered away to get clear; but the *Bismarck's* salvoes followed her out to a range of 10,000 yards. As the *Maori* retreated those on board her were sure they saw a torpedo hit. A bright glow seemed to illuminate the enemy's waterline and shortly afterwards another vivid glare appeared to betoken a second explosion. A cheer went up from the men on deck.

While the *Bismarck* was firing westward against the *Maori*, Captain Vian in the *Cossack* was engaged in attacking from another direction. He had been stealthily making his way up on her starboard side, and was now in a position whence he could take full advantage of her preoccupation with her other assailant. From the *Cossack*, the *Bismarck* was clearly silhouetted against the glare of her own gunfire, and at 1.40 a.m., only three minutes after the *Maori* had fired two torpedoes, Captain Vian fired three at an approximate range of 6,000 yards. After an interval, the *Cossacks* saw what they believe to be an unmistakable hit. Flames blazed up the *Bismarck's* forecastle,[1] visible not only to the *Cossack* but to all adjacent ships.

The *Sikh* had been driven off by the *Bismarck's* fire earlier in the night. Losing contact, she had taken in a report by the *Maori* that the *Bismarck* was steering south-west. It was probably a mistaken report for north-east, but it threw the *Sikh* out, and she went on for some time searching for the *Bismarck* in a south-westerly direction. Attracted, however, by the *Bismarck's* firing in opposition to the other destroyers' attacks, the

---

[1] A possible but unusual indication of a torpedo hit, which, by letting water into a ship, is seldom accompanied by fire.

Sikh was now on the way back. The *Zulu* had just reported the *Bismarck* as being stopped, and the *Sikh* believed that this provided an opportunity for a long-range attack. At eighteen minutes past two, she fired her four torpedoes at a range of about 7,000 yards. After an interval for the passage of the torpedoes, it was thought that there was the sound of an explosion.

Sikh and *Zulu* had now fired all their torpedoes, *Maori* had two left, *Cossack* one, while *Piorun* had not yet attacked. All the first four destroyers had withdrawn out of range after making their attacks.

The *Bismarck* seemed to remain stopped or was only steaming very slowly for an hour from 1.45 a.m. Some of the destroyers were not always in contact, but they knew roughly where the wounded battleship lay.

At about half-past two, there came a signal from the Commander-in-Chief, whose battleships were presumably not far off, for the destroyers to fire star shells to indicate the *Bismarck's* position. The Admiral was steering to get to the westward of the *Bismarck* for a dawn contact and was anxious for accurate knowledge of her position. His battleships and Captain Vian's destroyers had not yet been in sight of each other, and it was quite possible that, owing to natural variations of reckoning, the destroyers' positions relative to the flagship were appreciably different from what they purported to be. Moreover, the earlier succession of enemy reports had apparently come to an end an hour before. The firing of star shell by the destroyers might therefore give the Admiral a visual indication of the enemy's whereabouts. The destroyers began to comply with this order, but the unseen *Bismarck* quickly showed her resentment by opening an accurate fire on the star-shell firers; and Captain Vian did not think the Admiral would wish him to persist long with this explosive arrangement.

About 3 a.m., Captain Vian decided to take the *Cossack* in to fire her one remaining torpedo. The *Bismarck* was by now apparently under way again and proceeding slowly north-westward. Captain Vian worked round to the northward of her and, closing in, fired from about 4,000 yards. No hit was apparent,

The Destroyers Attack at Night

After this attack, all certain contact with the *Bismarck* seems to have been lost till shortly before 6 a.m. But Captain Vian was confident he would find her as soon as it began to get light. It was obvious that she was in an unhappy state. She had been steering a course which varied between north-west and north-east since 11 p.m., at a very low speed. She would not have been doing that on purpose. Therefore daylight was bound to reveal her whereabouts, and it was questionable whether it was sound to court too deliberately any more of her extremely accurate gunfire. At 5 a.m., Captain Vian ordered the *Piorun*, whom he knew to be short of fuel, to return to Plymouth. Commander Plawski, who had been much hampered by rain squalls, was then searching north-west for the *Bismarck*. He went on for another hour before regretfully shaping course away.

Direct touch was first regained by the *Maori*, who sighted the black shape of the enemy battleship at 5.50 a.m., Commander Armstrong making her out to be zigzagging slowly in a direction north-north-west at about 7 knots. Having found her, he shadowed her till daylight. Half an hour later, the *Sikh* sighted her emerging from a rain squall about three and a half miles away. Darkness was gradually giving way to twilight. Just before sunrise when the visibility was getting fairly good, the *Maori* determined to get rid of her last two torpedoes. She closed in somewhat and fired them from a range of 9,000 yards, just before 7 a.m. There was no hit, but once more the *Bismarck* opened fire and straddled several times. It was her last smack at the destroyers that had been snapping at her all night.

With the coming of full daylight, Captain Vian stationed his destroyers in four sectors all round the *Bismarck*, and they continued to keep her in sight. They had had a sleepless and tiring night, keyed up at high tension from dusk to dawn. Each destroyer had been under accurate shell fire from the *Bismarck's* heavy and lighter guns. All but the *Piorun* had indeed undergone that fiery ordeal at least twice and the *Cossack* had been through it thrice. They were frail craft and their officers and men were well aware that even one hit from the *Bismarck's* 15-in. guns would probably make an end of them. Considering how often

170

they had been straddled, it was astounding that not one of them had received a direct hit.

There can be little doubt that the periodical losses of contact during the night were mainly due to the accuracy of the *Bismarck's* radar-controlled gunfire. But for her ability to drive the destroyers outside sighting distance by this means, it should have been a fairly easy matter for them to keep her continuously in sight, had they concentrated on doing so. At the same time, an unexpectedly difficult shadowing problem was still further complicated by the fact that the destroyers did not give it their whole attention. The decision to carry out torpedo attacks could not fail to have a prejudicial effect on the business of keeping the enemy under observation. Successful shadowing calls for the avoidance of damage and the careful maintenance of a suitable shadowing position. The attack, on the other hand, postulates a deliberate exposure to damage and a period of high-speed manœuvring conducted with the single object of reaching a position for firing torpedoes, regardless of any other consideration. A shadowing destroyer which goes into the attack may emerge, if it emerges at all, five or ten miles from its shadowing station; and where, as in this case, the attacks are made piecemeal, the shadowing arrangements must soon be in disorder if not confusion. Shadowing and attacking by destroyers at night are, in fact, severely conflicting activities.

Nor does it seem that the hazarding of the primary object of shadowing was here compensated by the results achieved in pursuing the secondary object of attacking. It is true that several torpedo hits were claimed at the time. But according to the German records published by the British Admiralty, none were in fact scored.[1] The German statement to this effect may not, of course, be true. On the other hand, the receipt of torpedo hits would probably be known throughout the target ship, and the Germans would appear to have had no incentive to suppress

[1] 'The British Admiralty report that during the night attacks by destroyers of the Tribal Class torpedo hits had been scored on the *Bismarck*, damaging the engines, was not confirmed by statements of the survivors. According to these statements, the *Bismarck* did not receive any torpedo hits during the night.'— Fuehrer Naval Conferences 1941, p. 72.

the record of such hits, had they occurred. If anything, rather the reverse; and in the absence of such incentive, the German evidence that there were no hits could well be more reliable than the British belief that there were two. It is very difficult for destroyers attacking at night to be sure that their torpedoes have got home. The tell-tale pillar of water going up alongside the torpedoed ship cannot be seen in the darkness, and the boom of the target ship's own guns firing at the attacking craft can very easily be construed into the roar of an exploding torpedo. The force of suggestion is very strong on such occasions. The officers and men of the attacking ships want to see or hear a torpedo hit, and can quite genuinely convince themselves that they have done so when they have not. Especially is this so when they have been through danger and strain to achieve their attacks.

Moreover, the circumstances in which these attacks were carried out were unquestionably most unfavourable to success. A single battleship is a poor target for destroyers at night. It is still poorer when the destroyers are attacking separately and not as a group. Admittedly, a favourable factor in this case was the *Bismarck's* low speed, making quick avoiding action by her impossible. But against that were the long ranges at which many of the torpedoes were fired. To obtain good torpedo results against a single ship it is generally necessary to get in to about 2,000 yards before firing. Yet on this night, not one torpedo was fired at this range. Three were fired at 4,000 yards, four at 5,000 yards, three at 6,000, four at 7,000, and two at 9,000.

Why, then, did the destroyers attack from such ranges? Undoubtedly because they could not get in any closer, owing again to the great accuracy of the *Bismarck's* radar-controlled gunfire: that is to say, get in closer without grave risk of disablement or destruction. No doubt this risk would have been readily taken had it been a matter of slowing up the *Bismarck* at any cost. But Captain Vian had originally decided that, his primary object being to shadow the *Bismarck* and hand her over in due course to Sir John Tovey, he would not incur heavy losses in attacking. The position, therefore, appears to have been this: that while the shadowing was imperilled by the delivery of the torpedo

172

attacks, the torpedoes were fired outside effective range out of consideration for the shadowing. It seems an instructive example of the weakness inherent in pursuing two antagonistic objects at once, even though it be assumed that Captain Vian did not know beforehand what a formidable deterrent radar-controlled gunfire would prove to be. The endeavour to have the best of two opposing worlds is very likely to result in having the worst of both.

Once it had been decided that the *Bismarck* was probably crippled and was almost certain to be brought to action by the British battleships, the case for night destroyer attacks became a doubtful one. Had the *Bismarck* been steaming at speed towards Brest, then any action by the destroyers to slow her up would have been justifiable. But since she was moving away from it during most of the night, the need to reduce her speed hardly arose. Indeed, the faster she went in this favourable direction the better. It would appear therefore that there was no call on the destroyers to do other than shadow.

In the circumstances, the night was certainly not the best time to develop their offensive powers against the enemy. They were carrying out individual, unco-ordinated attacks at longish ranges and under adverse weather and sea conditions on an enemy ship who could use her whole armament in retaliation against them. Had they waited until the expected battleship action had been joined in the morning, the *Bismarck's* main and perhaps also her secondary armament would be fully occupied with her big-ship opponents, and the destroyers might well get in to close torpedo range without opposition.

Nor was the torpedoing of the enemy the only consideration for the destroyers to keep in mind. The screening of the British battleships against submarine attack would be a matter of importance next day, when the danger of U-boat attack would obviously have to be taken very seriously. It was, indeed, for this main purpose that the destroyers had been detached from their convoy and ordered to join the Commander-in-Chief. Yet the performance of this duty would clearly have been impeded, if not prevented, by damage incurred during the night attacks.

The Destroyers Attack at Night

It is, however, pertinent to note that Captain Vian's decision to attack was regarded with evident favour in the highest quarter at the time. Though he did not know it, the question of night destroyer attacks had already formed the subject of a communication from the Admiralty to the Commander-in-Chief. About 7 p.m., Sir John Tovey had received a signal, in a code the destroyers did not hold, asking whether he had considered ordering night destroyer attacks to be made. This signal, which the Commander-in-Chief can hardly have been over-pleased to get, was sent out before the *Ark Royal's* attack and therefore before the *Bismarck's* rudders had been hit. But it was not cancelled after the Admiralty must have become aware from intercepted signals that the *Bismarck* had probably been rendered unmanageable, nor after the reports of the destroyer attacks had begun to come through. It is therefore a fair assumption that Captain Vian's action in attacking had the full approval of the Naval Staff.

CHAPTER 11

The End of the Bismarck

To those on board the two British battleships, keyed up for approaching battle, the dawn seemed to be long in coming. Ships' companies were at action stations but were allowed, half at a time, to sleep at their posts. Neither of the two Captains left their compass platforms during the night, though each of them took an occasional doze, sitting in a chair and resting his head against some control instrument.

At last there came that faint awareness that the darkness was not quite as black as before, which meant that morning twilight was just beginning. Commander Robertson, the Admiral's Staff Officer (Operations) suddenly remembered that his steel helmet was down below in his cabin and he decided it was time he went to get it. As he went down the ladder into the cabin flat, an astonishing sight caught his eye. Round and round the flat were running in obvious terror four large rats. They took no notice of him but continued their frenzied roundabout, slipping and bumping into each other as the ship rolled. In the circumstances, it was not a very exhilarating spectacle, and Commander Robertson was glad to seize his helmet and get quickly back on deck.

Over in the *Ark Royal*, twenty to thirty miles away, the first aircraft shadowers had already been flown off. When they came up on the lift it was still pitch dark, and so strong was the wind down the flying-deck that the aircraft were seen to rise almost vertically past the bridge as they took off. As the daylight strengthened it revealed as stormy a scene as on the day before, while overhead there was the same mantle of ragged, leaden rainclouds driving across the sky. It was raining heavily and visibility was none too good.

Sir John Tovey was watching the weather conditions as they were gradually revealed. He had been up most of the night, examining the movements of the *Bismarck* reported by the destroyers. His main anxiety was how the destroyers' calculated positions corresponded with his. Neither his flagship nor the destroyers had seen the sun for several days and there was therefore plenty of room for errors of dead reckoning on both sides. It had been for this reason that the Admiral had told the destroyers to fire star shells in order to provide a visual bearing. But there was so much rain about that nothing was seen from the flagship and the firing ships reported they were being heavily shot at. The Admiral then ordered wireless transmission on medium frequency in the hope of obtaining wireless directional bearings. But for various reasons, this was no greater success than the star shells. As day began to dawn, the Commander-in-Chief was still full of uncertainty where his enemy was. This and the poor visibility of a stormy horizon convinced the Admiral that conditions were unfavourable for an immediate action, and that it would be better to wait an hour or two for full daylight.

Sir James Somerville had just come to much the same decision regarding the intended dawn air attack. In this vile weather, there was serious risk of the aircraft mistaking friend for foe, which made it prudent for this attack also to be postponed. Sir James was none too sure of the position of either the *King George V* and *Rodney* or of the *Bismarck*; and after the narrow squeak of torpedoing the *Sheffield* the day before, he wanted no more mishaps of that kind.

Shortly before sunrise, Sir John Tovey signalled across to the *Rodney* astern of him to tell Captain Dalrymple-Hamilton that in the forthcoming action he was free to manœuvre independently, provided he conformed generally to the Admiral's movements. The *Rodney's* two remaining destroyers had just been obliged to leave her for the return to their base for fuel. They had waited with her as long as they were able, but could wait no longer. Indeed, they had waited, as was to be shown later, rather too long.

The Commander-in-Chief's intentions, made known at this time to his Flag-Captain and Staff, were to close the enemy as quickly as possible to about 15,000 yards and then turn for a broadside battle. But first of all the *Bismarck* had to be located, and there was doubt as to her exact direction. The solution to this urgent problem was provided by the *Norfolk*. She had been rushing south in desperate haste all night, fearful of being too late for the final drama. At a quarter-past eight, she sighted a battleship about eight miles ahead and nearly end-on. Thinking it was the *Rodney*, Captain Phillips ordered the challenge to be made. Getting no reply, he had a more careful look and then realized that the vessel he was approaching at 20 knots was none other than the *Bismarck* herself. Once more the *Norfolk's* wheel was put hurriedly over, as it had been on the evening of the 23rd, three and a half days before, when she had run out of the mist in the Denmark Strait to find the German battleship also dangerously close.

As the *Norfolk* again sheered away to open the range, she sighted the two British battleships in the distance and was able to give them a visual link with the enemy. It showed Admiral Tovey that he was steering too much to the northward and he adjusted the course of his battleships accordingly. They were roughly in line abreast, a little short of a mile apart and were rolling considerably with the sea on the quarter. For Captain Dalrymple-Hamilton in the *Rodney* it was a family as well as a professional occasion, for his only son was a Midshipman on board the *King George V*.

At 8.43 a.m., the battleships sighted the narrow grey shape of a ship nearly end-on and about twelve miles almost ahead. It was the *Bismarck*. At last she was in sight. It was nearly a week since Sir John Tovey had first heard of her being in the fiord near Bergen; and during the long and anxious days that had followed she had seemed almost too slippery and elusive ever to be caught. But there she was now in front of him, cornered in the end. However, though she had been lamed and overtaken, none of her exceedingly sharp teeth had yet been drawn. There was the prospect of a sharp fight.

At 8.47 a.m., the *Rodney's* 16-in. guns opened the battle. Just as the salvo was due to fall, the *King George V's* guns flashed out and both the British battleships were in action. The *Bismarck* had not yet replied and she remained silent for another two minutes. Then she, too, joined in. 'Time of flight fifty-five seconds,' announced the Fleet Gunnery Officer on the Admiral's bridge in the *King George V*, as the *Bismarck's* guns went off, and he began to count out the seconds. But he was laughingly silenced by the Admiral, who said he preferred not to be given the exact moment when a 15-in. shell would hit him in the stomach. When the splashes went up, however, it was seen that it was the *Rodney* who was being fired at.

The *Bismarck's* first salvo was a long way short. But it did not take her long to correct her aim, and her third salvo straddled the *Rodney* and nearly hit her. Having been given latitude to manœuvre independently, Captain Dalrymple-Hamilton altered course to port and brought his A arcs to bear. Since he was under fire and the enemy might start getting hits at any moment, it seemed time to develop his full gunpower in retaliation.

Across the way, the *King George V* was steaming straight for the enemy in conformity with Sir John Tovey's belief in an end-on approach. The value of this manœuvre was not, however, about to be tested. The target ship was the *Rodney*, who had her broadside open, and the *King George V* remained unfired-at during the whole time she was pointing directly for the enemy. Since the *Rodney* was not part of the Home Fleet proper, Captain Dalrymple-Hamilton was unaware of Sir John's views about the end-on method of closing the range, or no doubt the *Rodney* would at this time have been steering a parallel course to the flagship. As it was, the *Rodney's* early turn to port to open her A arcs was subjecting the *Bismarck* to heavier gunfire than she herself could develop, and was also taking the two British battle-ships steadily farther apart.

The *Bismarck's* salvoes were continuing to fall near the *Rod-*

178

ney. But the latter, as well as returning the fire with all guns, was zigzagging to dodge the fall of shot, and no hits had yet come to her. At. 8.54 a.m., the *Norfolk*, who was six or seven miles to the north-east of the British battleships, opened fire with her 8-in. guns at 20,000 yards. The battleships' range was already closer than that and was shortening rapidly; and at about this time the *Rodney* brought her secondary armament into action. The *Bismarck* was now under the concentrated fire of three ships, and her own gunnery efficiency was noticeably falling off. From being regular and well-placed, her fire was becoming more and more erratic, and the *Rodney* was no longer seriously worried by it. It became known later that the *Bismarck's* main fire control position, the ship's gunnery brain, was hit and destroyed fairly early in the action, and it is possible that the marked deterioration in the volume and accuracy of her fire can be attributed to this cause. But the mass of shells now pouring in on her would have lowered her offensive power in any case.

Twelve minutes after the commencement of the battle, the *King George V* was in to 16,000 yards and Sir John Tovey thought it time to bring the flagship's full fire to bear. After a word up the voice-pipe to Captain Patterson to tell him what was coming, the Admiral made the signal for a course of south, nearly opposite to the very wobbly path the *Bismarck* was following. A minute before nine o'clock, the *King George V* began her swing to starboard towards the new course and her after turrets were soon in action. The *Rodney*, whose independent manœuvrings had by now taken her out to nearly three miles from the flagship, turned south two or three minutes later. She may or may not have taken in the Admiral's signal, but was under the instruction to conform generally to his movements. The *Bismarck* continued her slow course towards the north-west, yawing considerably each side of the wind. Just before the *Rodney* turned, Captain Coppinger saw a heavy shell burst on the *Bismarck's* forecastle, and gained the impression that one of her two foremost turrets had been put out of action. He was on the bridge with Captain Dalrymple-Hamilton, taking notes of the battle, and he made an entry to this effect.

The End of the Bismarck

Just after the turn, the *Bismarck* transferred her fire to the *King George V*, now the leading ship. But some of her guns were no longer firing and only an occasional shot or two fell close. On the British side, fire control had been difficult from the start. Against the dull, rainy horizon, the shell splashes did not show up at all clearly and it was hard to be sure of a straddle, more particularly with three ships mingling their salvoes round the one target. As the range decreased, the spotting of the fall of shot naturally became easier: but the turn to the southward introduced a new handicap. On that course, the resultant of the gale and the ship's speed gave a relative wind straight towards the *Bismarck*. Consequently, the clouds of brown cordite smoke that belched from the British gun muzzles at each salvo were hanging irritatingly in front of the firing ships, forming a semi-opaque screen between them and the enemy, to which the funnel gases added their quota. Fortunately, radar came to the rescue to some extent, but the fire control conditions were far from ideal.

A few minutes after the turn to the south, another British ship joined in the action from the eastward. This was the *Dorsetshire*. All night she had been coming up at her highest attainable speed, guided by the reports from the destroyers. She had, however, been obliged to turn into the wind about 2 a.m. and heavy seas had been steadily knocking her speed down, first to 25 knots, then to 20. Dawn came without her having sighted anything; but at 8.23 a.m., to Captain Martin's intense relief, the *Cossack* was sighted to the westward and course was altered in her direction. Twenty-five minutes later, gunflashes were sighted almost ahead, and very shortly afterwards the *Bismarck* was seen twelve miles away, firing at something to the westward. At four minutes past nine, with the range at 20,000 yards, the *Dorsetshire* opened fire. But owing to the many shots already falling near the enemy, observation of fire was very difficult, and fire was checked after nine minutes.[1]

---

[1] A survivor picked up by the *Dorsetshire* is said to have told Captain Martin that it was one of the *Dorsetshire's* shells which wrecked the *Bismarck's* fire control position. In view of the heavy concentration of fire against the *Bismarck* and of the fact that the survivors are most unlikely to have studied the battle obser-

180

May 27th

The run to the south by the *King George V* and *Rodney* went on for about a quarter of an hour, with the range nearly steady at 12,000 yards. Interference by cordite smoke, as already mentioned, was bad. The *King George V's* 5·25-in. secondary armament guns came into action a few minutes after the turn, but as they made the cordite smokescreen worse still, they were ordered to cease fire two or three minutes later. During this period, ten torpedoes were fired at the enemy, six by the *Rodney* at 11,000 yards and four by the *Norfolk* at 16,000 yards. None were seen to hit, and indeed it would have been a great fluke if any had done so when fired from such ranges.

This action on opposite courses naturally made the enemy's bearing draw fairly rapidly aft, and Captain Dalrymple-Hamilton decided to turn the *Rodney* round to preserve the broadside bearing and head the enemy off. The fact that the enemy's fire was now on the *King George V* would enable the *Rodney* to make her turn without danger, and at 9.12 a.m. the wheel was put over for the new course, Once round, the *Rodney's* full fire was again brought to bear at 8,500 yards, and she was thus able to cover the turn of the *King George V*, who came round some minutes after her.

Captain Dalrymple-Hamilton's decision to turn north on his own responsibility may seem to have been within the discretionary power allowed him to manœuvre independently. But, in fact, it was something more than that. A stipulated condition of that power was that he must conform generally to the Admiral's movements. By no reasonable standard could he be said to be so conforming if he turned north while his Admiral was continuing to the southward. In fact, though he doubtless did not realize it at the time, Captain Dalrymple-Hamilton was reviving the famous example set 144 years before by one Commodore Nelson at the battle of St. Vincent. Not since 1797 had a British battleship Captain turned out of the line of battle by his own decision until Captain Dalrymple-Hamilton did it on this occasion.

The *Rodney* was now the leading ship and, perhaps for that

---

vers' records, this statement can probably be explained by a prisoner's natural desire to ingratiate himself with his captors.

reason, the *Bismarck* made her again the target. Several of the enemy's shots fell very close, one being only a few yards from the starboard bow. In the *Rodney's* torpedo flat, twenty feet below the waterline, the torpedo tubes' crew had been listening to the sounds of battle over their heads. They could feel the ship shiver each time the heavy guns roared out a salvo, and the sounds of the enemy's shells falling in the water near the ship were unmistakable. It was a bit lonely sitting down there inactive amid the death-dealing turmoil, and the torpedomen were envious of the guns' crews busy with their job of raising and ramming home the huge shells and pushing over the levers that sent the great breech blocks slamming to behind the cordite charges. It had therefore been very welcome when the torpedo flat got the order 'action port' during the run south and for some time the torpedomen were hard at work loading and reloading the three-ton torpedoes into the tubes. Now after the turn, there were more thuds of enemy shells in the water, and one very loud metallic clang. The starboard tube had just been loaded, but the sluice valve door (between the tube and the sea) was found to be jammed and could not be opened. That one had been close.

The turn to the north by *Rodney* and *King George V* removed the nuisance of funnel and cordite smoke interference and enabled a good clear view at last to be obtained of the enemy ship. Both British ships were getting close, being in to 8,500 and 11,000 yards respectively, at which ranges details of the *Bismarck* were easily discernible through binoculars. Obvious signs of punishment were visible on board her. A fairly large fire was blazing amidships. Some of her guns seemed to have been silenced, and the others were firing only spasmodically. Her foremost turrets fired a salvo at 9.27, but shortly after that the *Norfolk*, who had placed herself almost ahead of the *Bismarck* for flank marking purposes, saw two of the forward 15-in. guns run down to maximum depression, as if a British hit had caused a failure of hydraulic power in the turret.

At lessening ranges, the two British battleships steamed north past the slowly moving enemy ship, pouring in a heavy fire from both main and secondary armament guns. At this relatively close distance hits on the upper works were easily seen. A large explosion occurred just abaft B turret (the upper of the two foremost turrets), which blew the back of the turret up over the bridge. Another and very spectacular hit blew away the 15-in. aloft Director, which toppled over the side. The *Rodney* fired another two torpedoes at 7,500 yards, but neither of them hit.

The unsteady crawl through the water to which the *Bismarck* had by now been reduced meant that the British battleships quickly overhauled and passed her, and soon the bearing had grown so far aft that the foremost guns were almost ceasing to bear. It would have been simpler to have shot the battle out on a more or less constant broadside bearing; but this could only be done by using approximately the same speed as the enemy. This was, however, much too low for safety in view of the probable presence of enemy submarines. The *Rodney*, therefore, began to zigzag close across the enemy's bows, firing sometimes at her starboard side, sometimes at her port and sometimes down the length of her hull. At the end of each of the *Rodney's* zig-zags, her foremost turrets would be on their extreme after bearing and firing close past the ship's bridge, where the blast was severely felt. On one occasion, it removed Captain Coppinger's steel helmet from his head with such force that it hit and knocked out a signalman standing some feet away. The former's notebook also flew out of his hand and disappeared, to be picked up later on the quarterdeck.

In order to keep well clear of the *Rodney*, the *King George V* had taken a broad sweep out and back on the enemy's beam. Moreover, she was by now (about 9.30 a.m.) suffering badly from the same complaint that had afflicted her sister ship the *Prince of Wales* in the earlier battle. Gunnery breakdowns were occurring with unpleasant frequency. Her three turrets were severally out of action from this cause for varying periods, one for as long as half an hour, while there were in addition several breakdowns at individual guns. There were times when her available firepower was down to 20 per cent of the maximum; a reduction which might, in other circumstances, have had disastrous con-

The End of the Bismarck

sequences. Fortunately, the *Bismarck* had by now been pounded almost into silence. Her after turret was still firing occasionally, but the others were dumb. Her A turret guns were drooping dejectedly downwards towards the sea; those of B turret were pointing starkly into the air on a fixed bearing. At the very close ranges to which her enemies had approached, hits were smashing into her one after the other. The *Norfolk* had been firing away all the time, and just before 9.40 the *Dorsetshire* joined in again from the north-eastward, the *Rodney* becoming aware of her presence by some of her 8-in. shells falling close ahead.

By 10 a.m. the *Bismarck* was a silent, battered wreck. Her mast was down, her funnel had disappeared, her guns were pointing in all directions, and a cloud of black smoke was rising from the middle of the ship and blowing away with the wind. Inside, she was clearly a blazing inferno, for the bright glow of internal fires could be seen shining through numerous shell and splinter holes in her sides. Her men were deserting their guns, and parties of them could be seen running to and fro on the upper deck as the shells continued to rain in, and occasionally jumping over the side, to escape by watery death from the terror on board. Captain Patterson would have ceased fire earlier had he known of this, but the *Bismarck's* port side was so often screened by a wall of shell splashes along her whole length that it was none too easy to notice what was happening on board her.

And her flag still flew. Ostensibly at least, she remained defiant. Though powerless and, like Sir Richard Grenville's *Revenge*, surrounded by enemies, she did not surrender: though under modern conditions the intention to surrender a ship is not too easy to indicate. Surrender or not, however, the British ships meant to sink her and as quickly as they could. At any moment, long-distance German aircraft might appear or torpedoes come streaking in from U-boats that were already quite amazingly late in arriving on the scene; while to add to the urgency there was the nagging anxiety of the acute fuel shortage. Both the *King George V* and *Rodney* should from this point of view alone have been on the way home hours ago, especially the former. There was absolutely not a moment to be lost in putting the *Bismarck* under-

184

water. Sir John Tovey's impatience showed itself by a desire for point-blank range: 'Get closer, get closer,' he began to tell Captain Patterson, 'I can't see enough hits.'

It was indeed astonishing that the *Bismarck* was still afloat after the battering she had received. She had been pierced and rent time after time by heavy and light shells from two battleships and two cruisers. She had been torpedoed by the *Victorious*, and by the *Ark Royal's* aircraft. The *Rodney* was now (10 a.m.) firing nine-gun broadsides at her from the 16-in. guns, the huge shells hitting her in threes and fours at a time. At 3,000 yards, the *Rodney* also fired her last two torpedoes, and one of them was seen to hit the *Bismarck* amidships.[1] The *Norfolk* had also fired her remaining four torpedoes from a range of 4,000 yards and believed she obtained at least one hit. But still the *Bismarck* floated.

The *Ark Royal's* aircraft had one more attack they could make, after which all their torpedoes would have gone. Vice-Admiral Somerville had intended sending them off at dawn. But, as already mentioned, there was so much rain and low cloud about that he was afraid of their mistaking the target. Sir James had been steering north towards the supposed position of the enemy, of whose exact whereabouts he was none too sure. However, at 8.10 a.m., the *Maori* was sighted ahead and gave the *Bismarck's* position as eleven miles nearly due north. At 0855, the distant boom of heavy gunfire was heard to the northward above the noise of the wind, and Sir James thereupon decided to send off the striking force at once.

It was just as ticklish a job as on the day before, but the twelve Swordfish got safely away at 9.26 a.m. They formed up and went off to the northward: and just as they disappeared ahead, the clouds began to break and from the *Ark Royal* they spotted first one and then another Focke-Wulf.

The striking force soon found the *Bismarck*, but also realized that an attack on her would be very hazardous. She was being fired at from both sides by four ships, and many of their shots were going very wide. At the very close ranges into which the British ships had now got, the trajectories of their shells were

[1] Said to be the only instance in history of one battleship torpedoing another.

The End of the Bismarck

were almost flat. A very slight error in aim, which the rolling of the ships would facilitate, would therefore take the projectiles that just skimmed the upper works of the *Bismarck* to a distance of two or three thousands yards beyond her before they struck the water. The result was that shell splashes were going up hundreds of feet into the air a long way from the enemy, which would have been death to any aircraft that had flown into them. The aircraft therefore flew on towards the *King George V* to ask for gunfire to be ceased while they went down to the attack. But beyond having some anti-aircraft shells fired at them, they received no attention.[1]

Meanwhile, Sir John Tovey was feeling acute concern at the refusal of the *Bismarck* to sink. He had given her a hammering by gunfire that he had no conception any ship could stand. But there she was, still above water. If she could bear all that without going down, who could tell how much more she might not endure? And Sir John was already quite certain that he could not afford to spend any more time on firing at this ship. It was imperative that his force should start back. He had waited dangerously long, as it was; and every extra half-hour would make his return more hazardous. He looked at the burning hulk, lying deep and sluggish in the water, that had once been a fighting battleship. It was obvious to him that whether she sank now or sank later, she would never get back to harbour. At 10.15 a.m., he signalled to *Rodney* to form astern on a course of 027 degrees (about north-north-east). He was going home.

As Sir John steered away, he signalled that any ship with torpedoes was to close the *Bismarck* and torpedo her. As it happened, the *Dorsetshire* was the only ship in the immediate vicinity with any torpedoes left. Captain Martin, however, had not waited to be told, but was already using them. At 10.20, from about 3,500 yards, he fired two torpedoes at the *Bismarck's* starboard side, one of which exploded right under the bridge. He then steered round to her port side and fired another tor-

---

[1] It is interesting to record that when Captain Patterson, who knew the mistake was being made, asked the officer responsible if he couldn't see the airmen waving at him, the officer replied he thought they were 'Huns shaking their fists'.

186

pedo from about 2,500 yards at 10.36. This torpedo also hit. The shattered leviathan, her colours still flying, silently heeled over to port, turned bottom up and disappeared beneath the waves. The time was 10.40. As she was turning over, Captain Martin received the Admiral's order to do what, in fact, he had already done. He at once made a signal to say that the *Bismarck* had sunk.

The great chase was over. The mighty *Bismarck* had been disposed of after a most gallant fight against superior force. All that was left of her were several hundred heads of swimming men, visible on the surface of the breaking seas. The *Dorsetshire* summoned the nearby *Maori* to help her pick up survivors. It was too rough to lower any boats, even had this been permissible. But lines were thrown out and jumping ladders let down the sides. Many of the men in the water were too exhausted to climb up them; but the *Dorsetshire* managed to haul eighty on board and the *Maori* thirty. Then came a lookout's report of a submarine periscope, and Captain Martin considered it high time to withdraw.

Just out of sight to the southward, Vice-Admiral Somerville had been listening for over an hour to the thunder of the unseen gunfire. It was taking surprisingly long to deal with the *Bismarck*. She was outnumbered and outgunned, and, if all was going well, it ought not to be taking all this time to sink her. At 10.25, he could contain his anxiety no further, and he signalled to ask Sir John Tovey if he had finished the *Bismarck* off. In reply, there came three signals in quick succession, each of them more unexpected than the last. The first said that the *Bismarck* was still afloat; the second that Sir John Tovey could not get her to sink by gunfire; and the third that Sir John was discontinuing the action through lack of fuel.

Unaccompanied as they were by any amplifying detail, these bald reports were capable of uncomfortable interpretation. Sir James Somerville's first thought was to ensure that the Swordfish striking force should get in an attack. He was drafting a signal to that effect when the *Dorsetshire's* signal came in that the *Bismarck* had gone down.

The End of the Bismarck

The air striking force did not get back from its abortive trip to the flagship in time to take part in the final sinking, and so returned to the carrier. In that weather, the aircraft could not risk landing on with their torpedoes in place, and they were ordered to jettison them into the sea. As they were landing on after doing so, a Heinkel III appeared out of the clouds and dropped a stick of bombs alongside. When all the aircraft were on board, Force H immediately set course for Gibraltar. Sir John Tovey's force was steering in the opposite direction. The moment the job had been done, the main hunting forces were separating as quickly as they had concentrated.

Force H made its way to Gibraltar without incident. One of its three principal units, the *Ark Royal*, had played a conspicuous part in the destruction of the enemy. But the ship's company of the *Renown* were sorely disappointed at their ship having taken no direct action against the enemy. They had come so far and got so near to the enemy, and it was galling in the extreme not to have fired a shot at her. They consoled themselves on the way back by telling each other that as the *Renown* had already been 'blooded' in the Mediterranean, Sir James Somerville had refrained from joining in the fray in order to give the Home Fleet ships, who had so far seen no action, a chance to distinguish themselves.

When Sir John Tovey's force had settled down to its return course, with its duty done and the tension eased, there were various departmental heads in all ships to be commended for their people's share in the successful result of the operation. Prominent among these latter were the engine-room complement of the *Rodney*. Her steaming performance had, indeed, been a notable one. She had had no proper refit since the war had started, and it was well known to the authorities that her machinery was in a highly parlous condition. She had been on her way across to America for a thorough overhaul when she was diverted to deal with the escaping *Bismarck*. Before she had sailed and any question of chasing the *Bismarck* had arisen, the Third Sea Lord had told the Director of Operations half jokingly that her boilers were in such a state that she would probably

188

come to a stop in mid-Atlantic and have to be towed the remainder of the way; and it has been mentioned in a previous chapter that her engines were having frequent breakdowns. Yet the *Rodney* had kept her place in the hunt, though it had meant several days of fast steaming culminating in thirty-six hours at full speed. Captain Dalrymple-Hamilton now wished to congratulate the head of the department, Commander (E) C. Burge on this fine effort, and sent down for him to come up on the bridge. The reply came back that Commander Burge had 'passed out'. He had been continuously below since the full speed began and had now fainted from strain and exhaustion.

As the *King George V* and *Rodney* left the scene of the action, they were joined by the *Cossack*, *Sikh* and *Zulu*; the *Maori* being behind with the *Dorsetshire* picking up survivors. The Naval Staff at the Admiralty had meanwhile been busy collecting together additional destroyers to meet the battleships on their way back, and eleven were already en route. It was, however, thirty hours before they joined up. During the critical period when the battleships were within reach of German aircraft and submarines, they had only the three vessels of Captain Vian's to screen them.

It was only to be expected that the Germans would make every effort to avenge the loss of the *Bismarck* by air attacks on the victorious British ships. But on the 27th only four aircraft approached the battleships, none of which achieved any hits. The main weight of the German air attack did not, in fact, fall on the big ships. It will be recalled that the *Mashona* and *Tartar* had hung on with the *Rodney* on the night of the 26th /27th as long as they possibly could. The result was that they were condemned to a slow-speed return to their base, the very contingency that Sir John Tovey had been so anxious to avoid for his battleships. In consequence, they had been overtaken and passed by the battle force and by dawn on May 28th were some 100 miles to the southward of it. In this position, they were discovered an hour or two later by a large body of German bombers, probably intended for an attack on the British battleships. The bombers decided to throw their main weight against the two destroyers. The *Mashona* was hit and sank about noon, with the loss of one officer and forty-five men.

She and the *Hood* were the only casualties in ships during the operation, and at 12.30 p.m. on the 29th the Commander-in-Chief reached harbour, with his oil tanks nearly empty.

CHAPTER 12

A Few Comments

The elimination of the *Bismarck* was undoubtedly a very important achievement, entirely justifying Sir John Tovey's belief, expressed in his message to his Flag-Captain and flagship on the evening of the final battle, that it would have an effect on the war out of all proportion to the loss to the enemy of one battleship. Had she been able to get clear away undamaged, the *Bismarck* might have been able to do very serious harm. The German U-boats were already causing grievous and mounting losses to the shipping bringing essential supplies to war-time Britain. One has frequently read that the Battle of Britain was the most decisive battle of the war for us, since had we lost it we should have been defeated. This fairly widespread view is not correct. The loss of the battle of the Atlantic would just as certainly, indeed more certainly, have brought this country to disaster; because not only should we have been reduced to practical starvation but we should have lost the stream of raw materials and finished products necessary for the production of the vast quantities of weapons and munitions required by modern war. Among other things, the Royal Air Force would soon have been grounded for lack of petrol;[1] and without petrol the Battle of Britain could not have been fought, nor the bombing of Germany carried out.

[1] Even such prominent men as Lord Trenchard do not seem to have realized this point. In a pamphlet issued by him in 1945 entitled *The Principles of Air Power on War*, he said: 'It should be recalled not only that we won the battle (of Britain), but that it was the only battle the loss of which could have meant the loss of the war.'

A Few Comments

If to Germany's already dangerous U-boat effort had been added the surface activities of the world's strongest battleship, the results might have been very awkward. Refilling her fuel tanks and shell rooms from oilers and supply ships using secret rendezvous, as she clearly meant to do, the *Bismarck* could possibly have kept at sea for weeks or even months, and while at large might have played havoc among the numerous convoys bound to and from the British Isles. The problem of giving these convoys adequate protection against the underwater offensive was proving difficult enough. That of providing protection against battleship attack was harder still. The number of convoys normally at sea at one time in the north and central Atlantic considerably outnumbered the British capital ships available to escort them; and of those capital ships a high proportion were old vessels incapable of standing up to the *Bismarck* on anything like equal terms. The odds were, therefore, that any convoy which the *Bismarck* came across would have a big-ship escort weaker than herself or no such escort at all. In such cases, she should have been able, especially if accompanied by a smaller vessel like the *Prinz Eugen*, to destroy the greater part of the convoy.

Nor would the material results of the *Bismarck's* escape have been the only factors in the case. Though battleships had been denounced for many years as obsolete anachronisms, the fact remained that their political potential was then still high. While the presence on the convoy routes of fifty to a hundred enemy submarines, taking a severe and increasing toll of merchant shipping, could leave the British public comparatively unmoved, the escape of a battleship from port was still in 1941 and later able to cause a stir in Press and Parliament. The appearance of the German battle cruisers *Scharnhorst* and *Gneisenau* at Brest a month or two before the *Bismarck's* dash had been the cause of a public uneasiness out of proportion to the damage they had done; of which latter, indeed, the British public was given no information. The safe arrival there or at some other French port of the bigger and more powerful *Bismarck*, especially after she had disposed of the *Hood* on the way, would undoubtedly have been a major sensation which could have had

192

11. H.M.S. *King George V* with H.M.S. *Victorious* astern

12. H.M.S. *Sheffield*

13. A broadside from H.M.S. *Rodney* falling near *Bismarck* during the final battle

14. *Bismarck* survivors in the water

incalculable political repercussions at a time when things were going badly everywhere. The sinking of the *Bismarck* is therefore to be regarded as an exceedingly fortunate occurrence.

The whole operation, moreover, which culminated in her destruction is of exceptional interest. If it was not actually the longest continuous chase in naval history—Nelson's pursuit of Villeneuve to and from the West Indies in 1805 covered greater distances—it was among the longest; while in point of dramatic reversals of fortune, of the frequent alternation of high optimism and blank disappointment, of brilliant victory followed quickly by utter defeat, it is probably unique in warfare. From the time the *Bismarck* and *Prinz Eugen* were first sighted in their Norwegian fiords to the time the *Bismarck* was sunk was three hours less than six days, during which the *Bismarck* covered nearly 3,000 miles and most of the British hunting forces not much less. Of that period, she was completely lost to sight and knowledge for three days and thirteen hours or more than half. During the two days and eight hours when she was in contact with British forces, she was attacked three times by heavy ships, three times by carrier aircraft, at intervals during the whole of one night by destroyers, and was finally finished off by torpedoes from a cruiser after being battered into a hulk by heavy gunfire; while she was shadowed by a variety of craft which included a battleship, three cruisers, five destroyers, and a number of Coastal Command and carrier aircraft.

It has been claimed by some people, including naval officers, that a special significance attaches to the fact that it was a torpedo from an aircraft that, hitting her rudders, slowed the *Bismarck* up and allowed her to be brought to action. It is true enough that without the intervention of the *Ark Royal's* aircraft the *Bismarck* would have got away. It is less well known that without a shell hit she received (probably from the *Prince of Wales*) in the action of May 24th the *Ark Royal* might have been unable to play her decisive card. This shell entered the forepart of the *Bismarck*, exploded deep down among some of the oil fuel tanks, and blew a hole in the ship's side. The effect was twofold. The hole allowed oil fuel to escape into the sea, the leakage of which caused that broad oil streak which was noticed for some time after the action by the *Suffolk* and the shadowing aircraft. It also let sea water into those particular oil tanks, thereby contaminating more oil that remained in the ship. The total result was that the *Bismarck's* supply of usable oil fuel was sensibly reduced and with it her capacity for continued high speed all the way to Brest. But for this hit, she could undoubtedly have maintained a higher average speed during the next three days, which could have put her, had she followed the same general course, two or three hundred miles closer to Brest when first sighted by the *Ark Royal's* aircraft; or probably just that much nearer home to have brought her to safety.

But without that shell hit, the *Bismarck* might well have decided to go on steering out into the Atlantic. Indeed, an Admiralty note to Sir John Tovey's dispatch says that it was this hit and the resulting loss of fuel which caused the German Admiral Lutjens on board the *Bismarck* to decide at 8 a.m.—or two hours after the action—to make for the French Coast.[1] It was presumably this decision which determined the *Bismarck's* alteration of course to south at 12.40 p.m. that same day, but for which alteration she would not have come within striking range of the *Victorious'* aircraft, and quite probably those of the *Ark Royal*.

The most correct conclusion to draw concerning the *Bismarck's* destruction is undoubtedly that it was the fruit of co-operative action on the part of numerous sea and air forces, the latter partly naval and partly R.A.F., all working in close accord for the one common end, and including all those surface vessels, submarines and aircraft which searched and patrolled without finding her. Without a Coastal Command flight, the *Bismarck* would not have been sighted in her Norwegian fiord. Without a Fleet Air Arm flight, her departure thence would not have been discovered. Without cruisers in the Denmark Strait, she would not have been sighted on her way through that passage at a time when shore-based flying was inoperative. Without heavy ships

---

[1] It is noteworthy that the Admiralty ascribed the hit to the *Hood*, though on what evidence it does not state.

to engage her next morning, she would not have been hit and her course brought round to where the *Victorious'* aircraft could torpedo her, and other forces get at her. Without Coastal Command and Fleet Air Arm aircraft she might not have been resighted after being lost. Without the aircraft from the *Ark Royal* she would not have been decisively slowed up. Without the destroyers, it would have been difficult to keep track of her movements during the night, and her rediscovery next day might have been too late for the battleships' critically low fuel supplies to allow them to engage her. And without the battleships, she would probably not have been sunk; for the *Ark Royal's* aircraft had torpedoes for only one more strike and the *Bismarck* could probably have withstood the likely extra torpedo hits well enough to have been towed home.[1]

Nor should it be overlooked that, for the unhampered use of her aircraft against the *Bismarck*, the *Ark Royal* was dependent on the close proximity of the battle cruiser *Renown*. The *Prinz Eugen* was still at large, and being an 8-in. gun ship was a more powerful vessel than the *Sheffield*, which latter was moreover away shadowing the *Bismarck*. Had the *Prinz Eugen* appeared and found the *Ark Royal* alone, she could have made mincemeat of her; and without any opposition from the *Ark Royal's* aircraft, which were otherwise engaged. The *Renown* was therefore very necessary for the protection of the *Ark Royal* against surface attack.

It is not always realized for what length of time a carrier can be virtually defenceless when her aircraft are on tactical employment. On this occasion, the *Ark Royal's* striking aircraft were either on reconnaissance, attacking, or refuelling and re-arming continuously from eight-thirty in the morning till ten o'clock at night; a whole day during which the *Ark Royal* herself was the most vulnerable vessel afloat, being a huge target with insignificant means of surface defence. It is possible, when contemplating the high offensive power of sea-borne aircraft, to forget the extreme weakness of the ship that carries them. Carriers are like

[1] Though the British submarines and/or Bomber Command might have got her on the way in.

A Few Comments

unarmoured battleships whose turrets are removed for hours at a time; and if they are to be the capital ships of the future, they must presumably have some form of surface protection during their periods of helplessness. It is one of the most interesting problems of naval strategy what size of ship could best provide it.

An impressive aspect of the operation is the very large number of hunting forces required to bring one battleship to book. Two enemy ships, one battleship and one cruiser, escaped from the North Sea into the Atlantic. The cruiser got clear away, for the *Prinz Eugen* was not sighted with any certainty after the loss of contact at 3 a.m. on the 25th and shortly afterwards was discovered in Brest by reconnoitring aircraft. The battleship was found and sunk; but to bring this about the following remarkable total of war vessels were from first to last involved: eight battleships and battle cruisers, two aircraft carriers, four 8-in. gun cruisers, seven other cruisers, twenty-one destroyers, and six submarines. In addition, there were numerous shore-based aircraft.

This imposing total provides a peculiarly striking illustration of the ample margin of superiority required by a Power that aspires to the command of the sea, or even of a portion of the sea. It also serves to emphasize how fortunate it was that the Germans sent their raiding heavy ships out by ones and twos. A few months before the *Bismarck* made her dash, the battle cruisers *Scharnhorst* and *Gneisenau* had escaped into the Atlantic and got to Brest. Some months after the *Bismarck* was sunk, her sister ship, *Tirpitz*, was fit for active operations. Had the Germans waited till the *Tirpitz* was ready and then sent all four ships out in company, the problem of dealing with them at sea would have been a thorny one indeed. But happily for us, the Germans decided to expend their capital ships in penny packets.

A point of some interest is whether the *Bismarck* should have turned back and returned to Germany after sinking the *Hood*. A triumphal return to a cheering Reich after a severe defeat inflicted on a superior British force which included the famous

A Few Comments

Hood would probably have produced a greater psychological dividend, both inside Germany and in the outside world, than any other course of action. Hitler himself seems to have thought this should have been done, for at his Naval Conference on 6th June 1941, the first question he asked was why Admiral Lutjens did not return to port after the engagement with the *Hood*. This inquiry may, however, have been no more than the attempt by a bitterly disappointed political leader to plant the blame for failure on to a naval subordinate. It was known in Berlin within an hour and a half that the *Bismarck* had sunk a battleship. If Hitler had then thought she should change her plans and return home, he could have told her.

Looked at from Admiral Lutjens's point of view, the case for a return to Germany was not too obvious. It is true that he had defeated the *Hood's* squadron with loss and it is probable that he, thinking the *Prince of Wales* to be the *King George V*, was unaware of any other naval intercepting force to block his way back to the Fatherland. Even so, he must have realized that there were powerful arguments against a return. Whatever effects that might have, it would not achieve the main object of the *Bismarck's* sailing—the sinking of enemy merchant shipping. She had been sent out for that very purpose; and Admiral Lutjens had been told, as the German naval archives show, to avoid if he could any risks which would jeopardize that object. However, if an encounter was inevitable, then an all-out engagement it should be. Well, there had been an all-out engagement, in which the *Bismarck* had done magnificently. But she had also been hit. It may quite well have occurred to Admiral Lutjens that, were he to turn back, there was always the possibility that the reason for this abandonment of his enterprise might be onpleasantly misunderstood. If, on the other hand, the Admiral took the *Bismarck* on, he would at least be carrying on with his original mission. There was only the question of damage repairs. These he could get done at Brest or St. Nazaire, if he could reach there: and after his victory of the early morning he probably assumed there was no adequate British force available to prevent him. He would, of course, be open to bombing attack while under repair. But he would also be subject to bombing attacks in the Denmark Strait on his return journey (if the weather happened to clear), and on his passage down the Norwegian coast to Germany. The British were now thoroughly on the alert and could be expected to be moving bombing squadrons northward to Iceland and Scotland to cover the chance of his doubling back. On the whole, there was a great deal to be said for going on. Whether or not this was Admiral Lutjens's line of thought, the action he took clearly had much to commend it.

The two principal British weaknesses—one strategical and the other technical—revealed by the operation related to fuelling and gun-mountings. The British effort to destroy the *Bismarck* very nearly came to grief on the rock of fuel shortage. The British fleet as an integrated force was quite incapable of conducting a prolonged chase. Ships were soon dropping out by ones, twos, threes, and fours, because their fuel supplies did not enable them to follow the enemy any farther; and we have seen how nearly Sir John Tovey had to abandon the pursuit altogether on the very eve of success.

The fact is that the Admiralty had consistently omitted, for many years, to give serious attention to the question of fuelling at sea. Had fast tankers formed a normal part of a seagoing 'task force', Sir John Tovey's ships could have oiled at sea and so have pressed on after the enemy without the increasing anxiety that they felt and the careful rationing of their speed that they were compelled to practise.

That no such organization existed in the British Navy can probably be ascribed to its two-century predominance among the fleets of the world having given it a copious supply of fuelling bases in every ocean. In consequence, British naval officers had become unduly 'base-minded', the shore stocks of fuel at one of Britain's numerous naval bases being uppermost in their thoughts when any question of mobility arose. The American Navy, growing to maturity at a time when most of the outside fuelling bases were in other hands, had long been accustomed to take its fuel and stores about with it. Later in the war, when the British fleet went to the Pacific where its own established bases had fallen into Japanese hands, it also had to adopt the American system and organize floating replenishments of every kind.

The other palpable breakdown was in the 14-in. turrets of the *King George V* and *Prince of Wales*. A new battleship needs a month or so to become efficient, if only because the ship's company require about that time to get to know their ship, become accustomed to their turret machinery, and perfect their gun-drill. It is even reasonable to find sharp edges which have to be filed smooth and other small mechanical defects in a brand-new ship. But after the 'shake-down' period, she should be a fully capable fighting unit. Neither the *Prince of Wales* nor the *King George V* showed herself to be so. Admittedly, the *Prince of Wales* had not undergone a proper working-up period. But this was not the main cause of her numerous and serious turret failures. The *King George V*, several months longer in commission, was almost as bad, her gunpower being dangerously depleted for long stretches during the action of May 27th through mechanical breakdowns. The truth was that there were faulty details in the design of their new-pattern 14-in. turrets. It is said that so many defects came to light during the *Bismarck* actions which would otherwise have remained longer concealed that more progress was made in perfecting the 14-in. turrets in the two months after the operation than would ordinarily have taken a year or more. In other words had the actions taken place in 1942 instead of 1941, the 14-in. turrets would probably have shown up nearly as poorly as they did on the earlier date.

These turrets were therefore manifesting the same characteristics that had marred most of their predecessors of the inter-war period. The new design of 8-in. turrets fitted in the County class cruisers took five years or more to make reasonably efficient. In their early years, they could seldom get off the eight rounds per gun of a practice shoot without falling to pieces. The same disease afflicted the new 16-in. turrets of the *Nelson* and *Rodney*, and they too were in process of adjustment and modification for five years or more before they could be pronounced fully fit to face an enemy. Had the new 14-in. turrets come out in peace-time, it is more than likely that they would have taken an equally long time.

To excuse and explain these long periods of semi-efficiency, the gunnery authorities of the Navy began to speak of them as being due to 'teething troubles' in new-design mountings. It was a very dangerous slogan, tending to obscure to those naval officers who should have had it most firmly in mind the cardinal fact that a new ship, if she is to fight at all, must be ready to fight at once and with all her armament. It is no use a ship steaming into action flying a kindergarten flag meaning 'I am still in the infancy stage. Please only fire half your guns at me'. The enemy, unfortunately, is unlikely to be so obliging.

By 1941, this 'teething trouble' slogan had got a serious hold in the Navy, as witness the remarks by the three officers most concerned on this occasion. Thus, Captain Leach of the *Prince of Wales* referred in his report of the action to '*the practical certainty* that owing to mechanical teething troubles a full output from the main armament was *not to be expected*'.[1] Again, Rear-Admiral Wake-Walker's dispatch spoke of the *Prince of Wales's* new turrets 'in which mechanical breakdowns had occurred and *were to be expected*'.[1] And the Commander-in-Chief himself could allude to her turrets which, 'of a new and untried model, were known to be liable to teething troubles. . . .'

In the pre-1914 days, the teething trouble catchphrase was unknown in the fleet. Yet new designs of turrets were appearing then as later. The 15-in. turret, in particular, mounting a calibre of gun never before used, came out during the first world war and was taken straight into action without any difficulty. Why, then, the complacent acceptance in the 1939 war of an inevitable inefficiency in new gun mountings which earlier generations had not tolerated?

The explanation is probably to be found in the naval limitation treaties of the inter-war period. Where a fixed limit is placed on warship tonnage, there is a natural tendency to squeeze into the treaty maximum as much as possible in the way of fighting power, resulting usually in the attempt to squeeze

[1] Author's italics.

too much. The endeavour to force ten guns into a ship that ought really to have had eight actually led to her having only six, since the ten had such complicated mechanism that no more than two-thirds of them would normally go off at once: or at all events for the first five or six years of the new mounting's life, until numerous modifications had been made in the light of breakdown experience. Similarly, elaborate arrangements to give new guns double the previous rate of fire would result in their producing half of it in practice. Mechanically, this sequence of cause and effect was bad enough. Psychologically, it was worse still; for the convention soon grew up that new gun mountings were bound to give poor results for some considerable time, while 'teething troubles' were being eliminated.

It is possible that the lesson of the 14-in. failures in action against the *Bismarck* has been taken to heart. But slogans, once coined, take a deal of discrediting; and that of 'teething troubles', in explanation of guns failing to fire, is one of the most insidious that the Navy has ever allowed itself to dally with. A motor firm that pleaded teething troubles in extenuation of frequent breakdowns in its products for the first five or six years of service would not last that length of time in business.

These blemishes were not the fault of the men who chased and sank the *Bismarck*. Indeed, they added to the merit of the achievement by multiplying the difficulties of bringing it about. An outstanding feature of that achievement was the number of the separate contributors. An unusually large proportion of the units involved were isolated vessels or small squadrons whose Captains or senior officers had mostly to make their own decisions about what they should do. These officers were given broad instructions by higher authority; but the interpretation of these instructions was mainly left to them and they generally had to act on their own responsibility in the light of their individual appreciations of what the enemy would do. It is a matter for remark how accurate their appreciations usually were and how well-judged the action taken in putting them into practice.

That they had the opportunity to display their skill was due not only to the nature of the operation but also to the readiness of the Commander-in-Chief, as the seagoing officer with chief responsibility, to leave them to their own devices, with the very minimum of direction. That the Admiral may have been influenced in this by his desire to forgo avoidable wireless traffic is certainly no more than one reason for his forbearance. He undoubtedly believed he could trust his subordinate commanders to do the right thing without being prompted by him; and the course of events showed that his trust was not misplaced. There could be no stronger argument for the principle of decentralization than the conduct of the outlying forces on this occasion; and no better example, since that of Nelson, of the willingness to decentralize by an admiral in command.

APPENDIX I

List of Flag Commanding Officers
(Decorations as held at the time)

HOME FLEET AND ATTACHED SHIPS

King George V	Admiral Sir John Tovey, K.C.B., D.S.O.
	Captain W. R. Patterson, C.V.O.
Hood	Vice-Admiral L. E. Holland, C.B.
	Captain R. Kerr, C.B.E.
Prince of Wales	Captain J. C. Leach, M.V.O.
Repulse	Captain W. G. Tennant, C.B., M.V.O.
Victorious	Captain H. C. Bovell.
Rodney	Captain F. H. G. Dalrymple-Hamilton.
Ramillies	Captain A. D. Read.
Norfolk	Rear-Admiral W. F. Wake Walker, C.B., O.B.E.
	Captain A. J. L. Phillips.
Suffolk	Captain R. M. Ellis.
Galatea	Rear-Admiral A. T. B. Curteis, C.B.
	Captain E. W. B. Sim.
Aurora	Captain W. G. Agnew.
Kenya	Captain M. M. Denny, C.B.
Neptune	Captain R. C. O'Conor.
Hermione	Captain G. N. Oliver.
Edinburgh	Commodore C. M. Blackman.
London	Captain R. M. Servaes.
Inglefield	Captain P. Todd, D.S.O.

203

List of Flag Commanding Officers

Electra	Commander C. W. May.
Anthony	Lieut.-Commander J. M. Hodges.
Echo	Lieut.-Commander C. H. de B. Newby.
Icarus	Lieut.-Commander C. D. Maud, D.S.C.
Achates	Lieut.-Commander Viscount Jocelyn.
Antelope	Lieut.-Commander R. B. N. Hicks, D.S.O.
Active	Lieut.-Commander M. W. Tomkinson.
Punjabi	Commander S. A. Buss, M.V.O.
Nestor	Commander C. B. Alers-Hankey, D.S.C.
Intrepid	Commander R. C. Gordon, D.S.O.
Cossack	Captain P. Vian, D.S.O.
Maori	Commander H. T. Armstrong, D.S.C.
Zulu	Commander H. R. Graham, D.S.O.
Sikh	Commander G. H. Stokes.
Piorun	Commander E. Plawski.
Somali	Captain C. Caslon.
Tartar	Commander L. P. Skipwith.
Mashona	Commander W. H. Selby.

FORCE H

Renown	Vice-Admiral Sir James Somerville, K.C.B., D.S.O.
	Captain R. R. McGrigor.
Ark Royal	Captain L. E. H. Maund.
Sheffield	Captain C. A. A. Larcom.
Dorsetshire	Captain B. C. S. Martin.

List of Aircrews
Sighting and Attacking the Bismarck

(1) *Victorious's* attack—May 24th/25th

A/C No.	Pilot	Observer	Air Gunner
5A	Lt.-Cdr. E. Esmonde, R.N.	Lt. C. C. Ennever, R.N.	P.O. (A) S. E. Parker
5B	Lt. (A) N. G. Maclean, R.N.	A/Sub-Lt. R. L. Parkinson, R.N.	Ldg Airm. A. L. Johnson
5C	Sub-Lt. (A) J. C. Thompson, R.N.	Mid. (A) L. Bailey, R.N.V.R.	N.A. D. A. Bunce
5F	Lt. P. D. Gick, R.N.	A/Sub-Lt. V. K. Norfolk, R.N.	P.O. (A) L. D. Sayer
5G	Lt. (A) W. F. C. Garthwaite, R.N.V.R.	Sub-Lt. (A) W. A. Gillingham, R.N.V.R.	Lt. (A) H. T. A. Wheeler
5H	Sub-Lt. (A) D. P. B. Jackson, R.N.	A/Sub-Lt. D. A. Berrill, R.N.	Ldg Airm. F. G. Sparkes
5J	Lt. (A) H. C. P. Pollard, R.N.	Sub-Lt. (A) D. M. Beattie, R.N.V.R.	Ldg Airm. P. W. Olitheroe
5K	Sub-Lt. (A) R. G. Lawson, R.N.V.R.	A/Sub-Lt. F. L. Robinson, R.N.	Ldg Airm. I. L. Owen
5L	A/Sub-Lt. (A) L. A. Houston, R.N.V.R.	Sub-Lt. (A) J. R. Geater, R.N.V.R.	Ldg Airm. W. J. Clinton

(2) Coastal Command Z /209's resighting of *Bismarck*—May 26th

Pilot and Captain	P.O. D. A. Briggs, R.A.F.
Second Pilot	P.O. F. W. Otter, R.A.F.
Navigator	F.O. J. C. Lowe, R.A.F.

Aircrews Sighting and Attacking the Bismarck

(3) *Ark Royal's* attack—May 26th

A/C No.	Pilot	Observer	Air Gunner
1st Sub-flight			
5A	Lt.-Cdr. T. P. Coode, R.N.	Lt. E. S. Carver, R.N.	P.O. (A) W. H. Dillnutt
5B	Sub-Lt. (A) W. S. Dixon-Child, R.N.V.R.	Sub-Lt. (A) G. R. C. Penrose, R.N.	Ldg Airm. R. H. W. Blake
5C	Sub-Lt. (A) J. W. C. Moffatt, R.N.V.R.	Sub-Lt. (A) J. D. Miller, R.N.V.R.	Ldg Airm. A. J. Hayman
2nd Sub-flight			
2B	Lt. D. F. Godfrey-Faussett, R.N.	Sub-Lt. (A) L. A. Royall, R.N.	A/P.O. (A) V. R. Graham
2A	Sub-Lt. (A) K. S. Pattisson, R.N.	Sub-Lt. (A) P. B. Meadway, R.N.	N.A. D. L. Mulloy
2P	Sub-Lt. (A) A. W. D. Beale, R.N.	Sub-Lt. (A) C. Friend, R.N.	Ldg Airm. K. Pimlott
3rd Sub-flight			
5K	Lt. (A) S. Keane, R.N.	Sub-Lt. (A) R. I. W. Goddard	P.O. (A) L. C. Mulliner
2M	Sub-Lt. (A) C. M. Jewell, R.N.		Ldg Airm. G. H. Parkinson
4th Sub-flight			
4A	Lt. H. de G. Hunter, R.N.	Lt.-Cdr. J. A. Stewart-Moore, R.N.	P.O. (A) R. H. McColl
4B	Sub-Lt. (A) M. J. Lithgow, R.N.	Sub-Lt. (A) N.C.M. Cooper, R.N.V.R.	Ldg Airm. J. Russell
4C	Sub-Lt. (A) F. A. Swanton, R.N.	Sub-Lt. (A) G. A. Woods, R.N.V.R.	A/Ldg Airm. J. R. Seager
5th Sub-flight			
4K	Lt. (A) A. S. L. Owen-Smith, R.N.	Sub-Lt. (A) G. G. Topham, R.N.V.R.	P.O. (A) J. Watson
4L	Sub-Lt. (A) J. R. N. Gardner	Sub-Lt. (A) J. B. Longmuir, R.N.V.R.	
6th Sub-flight			
4F	Sub-Lt. (A) M. F. S. P. Willcocks, R.N.	Sub-Lt. (A) H. G. Mays, R.N.	Ldg Airm. R. Finney
4G	Sub-Lt. (A) A. N. Dixon	Sub-Lt. (A) J. F. Turner, R.N.V.R.	Ldg Airm. A. A. Shields

206

Movement Diagrams
and
Battle Plans

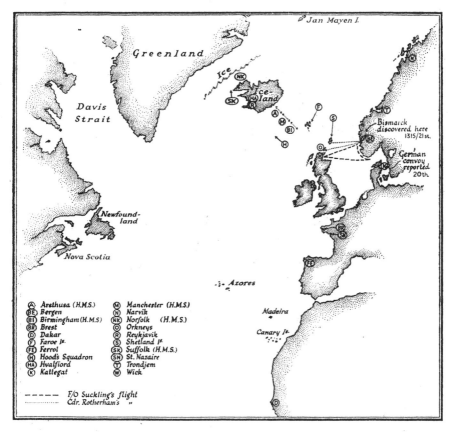

1. Key map of the general strategical area involved in the operations against the *Bismarck*, as at 10 p.m. on May 22nd, 1941

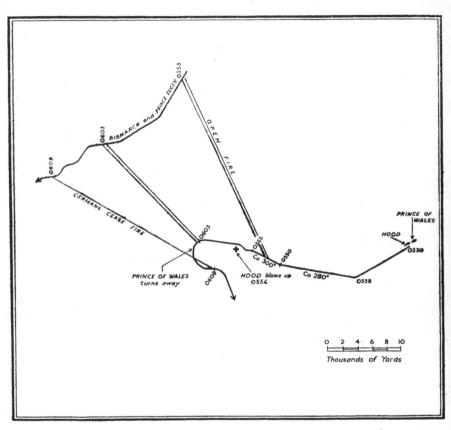

2. Plan of the action between the *Hood* and *Bismarck* squadrons on May 24th, 1941

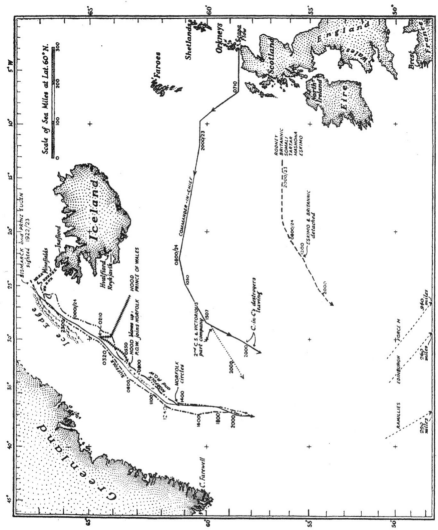

3. Ships' movements
up to 10p.m. on May
24th, 1941

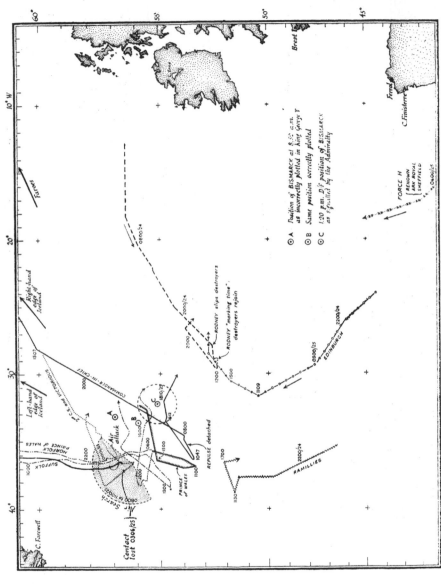

4. S h i p s '
movements up
to 10 p.m. on
May 25th

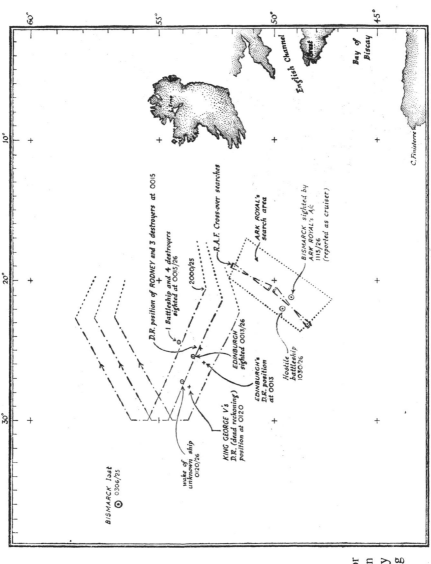

5. Air searches for the *Bismarck* on the night of May 25th and morning of 26th

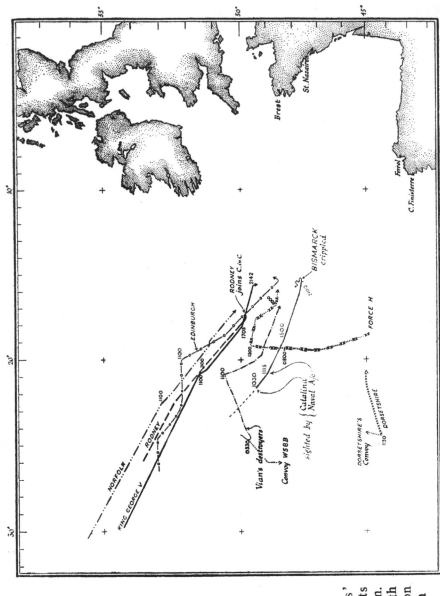

6. Ships' movements from 10 p.m. on May 25th to 10 p.m. on May 26th

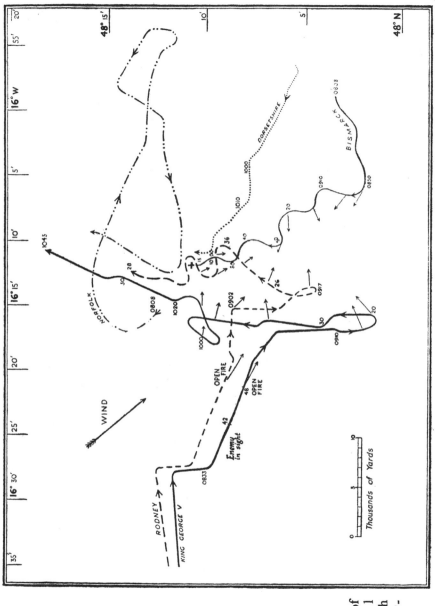

7. Plan of
the final
action with
the *Bis-
marck*

Index

Index